MANUAL DEL BARATERO,

ó

ARTE DE MANAJAR LA NAVAJA,

EL CUCHILLO Y LA TIJERA DE LOS JITANOS.

The Manual of the Baratero,

or

the Art of Handling the Navaja,

the Knife and the Scissors of the Gypsies.

A transcript and translation
by James Wran

MANUAL

DEL

BARATERO,

ó

ARTE DE MANEJAR LA NAVAJA,

EL CUCHILLO Y LA TIJERA DE LOS JITANOS.

WITH MANY THANKS TO

My dearest wife, partner, and best friend, without whom I could never have come even close to achieving my dreams.

Lois Spangler: for assistance with editing, translating more complex and culturally unique sections.
Keith Myers: for discussions on blade arts.
Oscar Reyes: for discussions on cultural blade arts.
Aidan Hughes: for assistance accessing scans of supporting documents.
Chris Slee: for assistance with publication and French translations.

There are many others who have supported and inspired me on my journey in the martial arts. Each have had untold yet deeply appreciated influence. Many in the Australian HEMA community have been students, but all have been teachers.

Manual del Baratero, or the Art of Handling the Navaja,
the Knife and the Scissors of the Jitanos

Translated by James Wran

Copyright 2020 © James Wran

All rights reserved. This book may not be reproduced in any form in whole or in part without permission of the author.

To contact the author:
jameshwran@gmail.com

Ravensword Press

ISBN: 978-0-6489723-0-3

Neither the author, nor the publisher, shall have any liability with respect to use or misuse of information contained herein. This work is intended as a reference only.

CONTENTS

Prologue

About the Manual del Baratero

 The Author: MdR

 The Artwork

Cultural context: setting the scene

 Blade culture in Spain

 The art of the *navaja*: where did it come from and where did it go

 The *Baratero* and the *Jitanos*

 Language

The transcript and translation

Appendix: Contemporary sources

 L'Espagne, Davillier & Dore

 Zincali, George Borrow

 A Handbook for Travellers in Spain, Richard Ford

 Others

Glossary

End Notes

Bibliography

PROLOGUE

This project began as a translation along with the idea of a 'how to' training manual. The translation itself became a deep rabbit hole of delving into historical documents. The training manual proved to be a larger task than I first thought and deserving of greater attention. I wished to share this translation and my love of the b*aratero* style. The training manual will follow later.

The motivation for this translation of the *Manual del Baratero* was threefold. Having trained in the martial arts since the age of 8 I have held an interest, and trained in, various martial arts. This began with open hand arts, but moved on to the use of various historical weapons.

As far back as I can remember I had an interest in historical weapons, especially the sword, and in time became an instructor of Historical European Martial Arts (HEMA). I found myself translating a late 16th century manuscript by Filippo Vadi from Pisa, Italy. From that process I learned a great deal more than just the techniques, gaining an insight into the author as well as the social context of the time.

There have always been family stories that a part of my ancestry came from Spain, accompanied by tales of my great grandmother living far out in the Australian bush on a sheep property, who used to throw knives, very skillfully, around the kitchen when she was of a temper. The romance and intrigue of some connection, true or otherwise, to the *gitanos* has always brought me joy.

Upon my first reading of the *Manual del Baratero,* I immediately loved the aesthetic and style of the *navaja;* the intricacies of the blade reflecting the nature of its use and those who wielded it.

Understand that the *Manual del Baratero* is not about learning how to fight with a knife, rather it is a window into the history of the ways of personal combat, the culture of the *baratero,* and the social context of Spain in the mid 19th century. The techniques and ideas can certainly be fun and provide ways to develop some applicable martial skills such as distance, timing, agility and deception. However if your aim is only to learn to knife fight then there are surely more relevant and efficient ways to learn and to practice.

Part of my interest in historical martial arts have been the use of what is now known as the rapier. Whilst my primary area of study and teaching is from Italian Renaissance and Elizabethan Masters such as Vincentio Saviolo and Giacomo di Grassi, I have spent many joyful hours crossing blades with those who study *La Verdadera Destreza* and its common and vulgar predecessor arts.

I have always found a deep interest in the history of martial arts, of how the physical techniques, principles and tactics have developed, moved, and changed through cultures, places, and times. The arts of the *navaja* are just another step along that journey. The aim of this book is to provide a translation and some insight to the period. I hope that the reader shares some of the joy in discovery of the art of the *baratero*.

ABOUT THE MANUAL DEL BARATERO

Little appears to be known about the *Manual del Baratero*, printed in 1849 by D(on) Alberto Goya. Scans of the original are available online, with hard copies held by University of Wisconsin, and in the National Library of Spain.

Whilst it does provide lessons and describes the use of the *navaja*, and the *baratero* who carry it, the *Manual* is certainly not a technical instruction book. The descriptions most often are ambiguous, likely with some assumed cultural knowledge and language from the time. The Manual has the feel of exaggeration and presents a somewhat romanticised idyll of the *baratero* and their culture.

It could be argued that the *Manual* was written by someone with very little experience in the use of the knife. The technical descriptions, whilst sometimes clear and concise, can also be confusingly ambiguous, and most often incomplete. There is also very little if any tactical information around the use of the *navaja*. It is clear that the information shared is only a brief overview rather than a comprehensive how to.

A reader could be forgiven, upon only a brief reading, for thinking that the *Manual* has no real value regarding the use of the knife. However it holds a special place in a compendium of sources describing the art of fencing with the knife. What the *Manual* describes is clearly an important step in bringing to a modern audience those skills which most likely were hidden within traditions never before put into writing.

The *Manual* may simply have been a curious little book designed to carry social commentary and likely as a way for the author to make some quick coin. Such publications were a popular genre amongst Spanish and wider European society, as evidenced by the numerous titles and travelogues at the time.

Whatever the reason for its creation the *Manual del Baratero* does depict a snapshot of the life of the *baratero* and the significant blade culture of Spain. It provides a starting point through which we can bring to life the art of the *navaja*. Through some understanding and research into Spanish sword arts of the time such as common or vulgar fencing, and *La Verdadera Destreza*, a more complete picture can be discovered of the place of importance for the various blades of Spain, from small knife to long rapier[1]. More hints at the importance of blade in Spanish culture can be seen in the supporting documents (see Appendix).

THE AUTHOR OF MANUAL DEL BARATERO

Most references to the *Manual del Baratero* note the author as *Anonimo*, or Anonymous. At the end of the Prologue are the initials 'M. d. R.'. It is possible that these are the initials of the author of the *Manual*, or simply the one who wrote the Prologue. It is conceivable that the author may even have been playing off the popularity of another prolific author of the time. If this be the case, there are numerous potential contenders. Here are two.

Mariano de Rementería y Fica, was born 7th April 1786 in Madrid, and died 5th December 1841. Rementeria was a journalist, newspaper editor, translator and author. He wrote, among others, similarly titled "*Manual del...*" styled books, which seemed to be a popular genre at the time. The *Manual del Baratero* was published 1849, after his death.

Some of the books written by Rementaria are:
- *El Hombre Fino al Gusto del Día.* (1829) (The Refined Man According to Today's Tastes)
- *Manual alfabético del Quijote* (1838) (Manual of Don Quixote in Alphabetical Order)
- *Conferencias gramaticales sobre la lengua castellana* (1839) (Grammar lectures on the Castilian / Spanish language)
- *Poesías* (1840) (Poems)
- *Manual del cocinero, cocinera, repostero, pastelero, confitero y botillero* (1851) (Manual of the chef, cook, pastry cook, baker, confectioner and *botillero*)[2]

While there are numerous enticing connections between the initials *MdR* and Rementeria, unfortunately there is no direct evidence of authorship. Numerous books were reprinted after Rementeria's death, and the *Manual of Cooks* continues to be reprinted to this day. A review of scans of Rementeria's works held in various university libraries show some similarities with *Manual del Baratero*, but no distinct evidence to link the *Manual* to the other books. There is also no evidence of other Rementeria titles printed by Alberto Goya. There is only a little evidence of Rementeria being a fighting man, having returned to Bilbao to take up arms against the French invaders during the Peninsular War of the Napoleonic Wars[3].

Social commentary is commonplace through Rementeria's writings, as are discussions on customs and language. Interestingly there are some small references to 'fine gentlemen' and 'confectionery bakers' in the *Manual del Baratero*, providing some connection to other published works.

James Loriega in his translation of the *Manual* (2005) claimed it as common knowledge that The *Manual del Baratero* was written by Rementeria, but provided no evidence.
There were internet rumours of a printing of the *Manual* which clearly showed the author to be Rementeria, but I am unable to find any evidence of another, possibly earlier, edition.
A modern edition of the *Manual* was published by Heliodoro (Madrid) in 1980 and attributed to Rementaria. This was an "Edition enriched

with six engravings by Gustav Doré" which may have added to confusion about the author and artist.

Another possibility is that the *Manual* was written by the poet from the end of the *Manual*, Don Manuel Breton de los Herreros (1796 – 1873). Herreros was a prolific playwright, poet and a journalist in Madrid. He spent time in the military, enlisting to fight the French in 1812, attaining the rank of corporal by 1822, and later becoming a civil servant for the liberal government. It is reasonable to assume that he had some experience of fighting. Herreros' liberal views would account for the social commentary in *Manual del Baratero*, especially considering the political atmosphere of the Carlist Wars at the time. There are numerous references to corporals interacting with the *baratero*, and Herreros' poem at the end has some marked similarities to the writing in the Manual.

Enticing speculation but it's still no evidence.

THE ARTWORK

As with other historical weapon treatises the imagery included must be given some consideration regarding its veracity and value. Some sections specifically refer to the images in the book, which are rudimentary at best. It is by no means an illustrated step by step instruction manual, and the images appear to be added for flavour rather than education.

Gustav Dore (1832 to 1883), a prolific French artist, made numerous illustrations of the *baratero* and the use of the *navaja*, many of which were included in Davillier's *L'Espagne* (see Appendix). Sadly the artwork in the *Manual del Baratero* was not done by him, as he would have been only 17 at time of publishing. Fortunately his art (see Appendix) actually provides much greater insight into the use of some techniques than the *Manual* does.

CULTURAL CONTEXT: SETTING THE SCENE

By the time of publication of *The Manual del Baratero* the Spanish people lived with memories of the greatness of the Spanish Empire as the world's leading power through the 16th and most of the 17th centuries. The 17th saw a steady decline, followed by hostile occupation and civil wars into the 18th century. The early to mid 19th century in Spain was a time of significant social upheaval and unrest which would lead to further violence in the near future.

A brief snapshot of history leading up to the 19th century:
- **1469**: The Kingdoms of Castille and Aragon were united by the marriage of Isabella I of Castille and Ferdinand II of Aragon.
- **1492**: Christopher Columbus discovered the Americas.
- **1500s** to late **1600s**: rise and fall of the Spanish Empire.
- **1704** to **1714**: War of Spanish Succession
  - The establishment of a true Spanish state by Philip V (reigned 1700-1746) saw a gradual recovery and growth in prosperity.
- **1793**: war against the French Republic.
- **1807**: Alliance with France and the Napoleonic occupation of Spain; Joseph Bonaparte placed as monarch 1808 to 1813.
  - The Napoleonic War economically ruined and divided Spain.
  - Joseph Bonaparte was replaced by Ferdinand VII after many Nationalist uprisings and the development of a constitutional monarchy.

- **1809**: Spanish colonies in America began to revolt and declare independence.
    - Spanish American Wars of Independence 1808 to 1833.
- **1821**: Mexico declares independence.
- **1833** to **1876**: a time of civil war between the Carlists (supporting the Spanish traditions of Catholicism) and Legitimism (the Monarchy succession of the French Bourbon dynasty), against the supporters of liberalism and republicanism. This began in 1833 when Ferdinand VII died and left his wife Maria Cristina as Queen Regent, supported by the Liberals, on behalf of infant Isabella II.
    - Continual unrest in Spanish colonies in the Philippines.
    - First Carlist War 1833 to 1840.
    - Second Carlist War 1846 to 1849.
- **1868** Spanish Revolution.

Throughout this history there was a continuation of regional, socio-political, and cultural separation of the old kingdoms (Castille and Aragon), with a mixture of cultures and languages, including the Catholic Christian and Islamic faiths, European culture in the north, and African culture in the south, as well as the divide between the wealthy and the poor. All this provided ample breeding grounds for a knife culture and the people that used them.

BLADE CULTURE IN SPAIN

The blade has been associated with Spain throughout its history being full of war, colonisation, expansion, and civil uprising, perhaps due to its central place between Europe and Africa and the movement of peoples and culture. From the Celto-Iberian swords, the mysterious sword of Hannibal, the Roman defeat by and adoption of the *gladius hispaniensis*, the legends of Toledo steel, the fabled *Tizona* sword of El Cid in the 11th century, coalescing through the long periods of warring between the kingdoms of Castille and Aragon, to the of the growth and decline of the Spanish Empire, Napoleonic takeovers and the Carlist civil wars.

As can be read in the supporting document extracts (see Appendix), it is clear how integral the blade had become to Spanish culture by the 19th century, and this was well known across other cultures as well. Richard Ford in his *Handbook* tells us that the use of the knife of the man on the street was much more practiced and perfected than that of the surgeon. (Ford, 1845)

The *Manual del Baratero* talks of how:
> "since very distant times there are men who carry the pompous title of Senior Master of the Kingdom, others who are called Second Lieutenants, and finally the simply named Master of Arms"

Tim Rivera in his translation of Godinho tells us that:

"records of fencing masters in service to the various, Iberian royal courts extend back to at least the early 15th century. In 1478, their Catholic Majesties Fernando and Isabella established the office of *maestro mayor* (senior master) to be the chief examiner of fencing masters." (Rivera, 2016)

Clearly the blade, either sword or knife, and its skillful use, had become commonplace in Spanish society well before and continued throughout the 19th century.

WHERE DID THE ART OF THE NAVAJA COME FROM?

The use of small utility blades, and combat with knives, has arguably been around since very early times, with depictions of such from Egypt, Greece, Rome and many other places across the globe. Actual treatises, depicting the use of and defence against the dagger, exist from as early as the beginning of the 1400's.

It is reasonable to assume that any bladed weapon arts existent in Spain by the 19th century had been influenced by the earlier arts and principles, codified and written about by fencing masters. from as early as 1474 by Jaime Pons. Similarities of the art of the *navaja* to vulgar, or common, fencing are reasonably obvious, even with only brief review of treatises such as Godinho's from 1599. Similarities are seen in footwork, circular movement, fingernails up and down in the grasp of the blade, and language used to describe various actions. Even the most basic of technical proficiency would have been passed to soldiers, made up at least in part by common folk.

The impact of later treatises from the *verdadera destreza* tradition can neither be quantified nor denied. The principles of nobility and status may have provided some obstacle. However the concepts of honour are definitely apparent in the art of the *navaja* and the life of the *baratero*, if somewhat differently expressed. It is unlikely that similar principles and skills in combat would develop in isolation in such close proximity.

Egerton Castle believed this to be true, stating in his book *Schools and Masters of Fence from the middle ages to the eighteenth century* (1885):

> "Among the commoner devotees of the art of fence superiority began to be sought in the management of the dagger, when the monopoly of the sword was assumed by their betters.
>
> To this we may ascribe the origin of the art of wielding the *navaja* – the long Spanish knife – which, when practised with the *capa*, was based on the principles of ancient sword-and-cloak play, and when alone, on those of the single rapier according to Carranza's teachings."

There are hints that this 'monopoly of the sword' stemmed from a limitation upon who could carry a sword. In order to find detail on such licensing laws many hours would be required, delving through numerous ancient handwritten Spanish Decrees. Denis Cherevichnik gives a tantalising possible reference to Ch 24 of the *Nueva Planta* Decree of Filipe V, released 16 January 1716. Unfortunately this document, whilst available online, has not been transcribed from its cursive form and is some 400 pages long, so an exact supporting reference cannot be provided.

> "As a result, it was possible to find out that, according to chapter XXIV of the royal decree of Philip V of January 16, 1716, the right to wear a sword was granted only to representatives of Nobility, to persons who were granted special privileges, as well as to those who received a special license. Thus, we must admit

that, in any case, Sir Egerton Castle was right in this: at the beginning of the XVIII century, the lower classes of Spain finally lost their swords and, apparently, were forced to look for a relatively legitimate alternative." (Cherevichnik, 2018)

There were also significant restrictions under martial law on the carrying of weapons, including scissors and knives, in Spain during the Peninsular War and Napoleonic occupation in the early 1800's.

"Thus ended the famous revolt of the Dos de Mayo. As far as such tumults went, it had not been particularly impressive, but for all that it was to have profound effects. In the first place, the fighting was replete with images of popular heroism and French brutality: many of the insurgents had fought with little more than their bare hands; the dead included a number of women, including, most famously, a young girl named Manuela Malasaña who was shot dead at the artillery depot; and it was rumoured that even possessing a pair of scissors had been enough to procure a death sentence. As Foy admits, 'Among those who were condemned were men who had not fought, and whose only crime was that of having large knives, or other sharp instruments. They were executed without the assistance of a priest… a circumstance which still more exasperated a religious people." (Esdaile, 2003)[4]

All this giving further growth to a knife culture particularly amongst the people of the streets.

WHERE DID THE ART GO?

Similar knife arts, techniques, principles, and even blade shapes, can be seen in the arts of other places around the world. Spain had considerable influence across the world for a long period of time through empirical expansion and colonisation, most often bringing with it the arts of war and violence.

It would be reasonable to see similarities adopted into local martial styles. A most obvious example is in the Philippines, the practice of *spada y daga* and other fight styles with stick and knife. Direct attribution is mostly conjecture however it is of interest to consider the similarities and possibilities.

Following the rise and fall of Spanish colonisation the Bowie knife appeared, and was made famous through Mexico, Texas, and Arkansas. It has a similar blade shape to the *navaja*, and techniques of use. Old newspaper articles such as *Six Inches of Steel*[5] show strong similarities in usage and tricks.

In Portugal and the South Americas *escrima criolle* and the *gauchos* also have similar shaped blades, described actions and techniques. There is a strong history of the use of the knife among traders, dock workers, smugglers, criminals and the lower social classes, and many had Spanish cultural backgrounds.

Other treatises such as the French *Defence in the Street* by Emile Andre[6] also reveal similarities of tricks and management of the knife. Andre in fact mentions the use of the *navaja* in Spain; quite possibly a connection through reading Davillier's *L'Espagne*, or even the *Manual del Baratero* itself (see Appendix).

Finally, there are many interesting similarities between the language and techniques of the *baratero*, and the use of the *navaja*, and those of current day bull fighting, and the dancing traditions of tango and flamenco, however this exploration is beyond the scope of this project.

THE BARATERO

The *baratero* and their world are richly described in the *Manual* and the supporting *L'Espagne* (see Appendix). The word *baratero* has connections to a person who buys and sells goods, in the marketplace and on the street, along with the art of haggling and bartering. However, the label of *baratero* became much more well-known as applying to the underclass, living a life of crime, swindlers, gamblers, smugglers, ruffians, scoundrels, thugs, and tricksters. The *Manual* clearly depicts three types of *baratero*;

> those who run gambling dens and take, often forcefully, a cut of the proceedings, those amongst the soldiers, living like kings and bishops, those in the jails, known for their violence.

> Another source: "a man of the dregs of society who has acquired extraordinary skill in handling knives and who exploits the terror he inspires to demand of gamblers a share of the purse."
> (Davillier, 1874))

THE JITANOS

The name *jitanos*, like the anglicised *gypsy*, is the pejorative for those of the Romani culture, incorrectly assumed to have come from Egypt, also known as peoples travelling across the globe and existing in many countries, most often with the reputation as clever and cunning travellers, nomads, tricksters, card readers, horse sellers and so on.

It must be clearly stated that the terms *jitano / gitano*, and *gypsy* are derogatory, and used in this text only for clarity and as a reflection of the original *Manual* and supporting documents.

The *Manual del Baratero* refers specifically to the *jitanos* using the scissors or *tijeras* most commonly associated with those who serviced, managed and maintained horses, livestock, and trade caravans.

As a point of interest the poet *"Demófilo"* identified the flamenco with the gypsies. *"The gypsies,"* he wrote, *"call the Andalusians gachós, and these call the gypsies flamencos."* [7]

> "His summing up of this relationship between the popular and the gypsy is worth quoting: The gypsy *cantes* ... Andalusianising themselves, so to speak, or becoming *gachonales* ... will continue gradually to lose their primitive character and originality and will become a mixed genre, which will continue to bear the name of *flamenco* as a synonym for gypsy but which will be basically a confused mixture of heterogeneous elements.
> (Smith & Ingelmo, 2012)[8]

LANGUAGE

The *Manual del Baratero* is very close to modern Spanish with a spattering of Andalusian and Caló (spoken by the *jitanos*) referred to in the *Manual's* final prose as being the manner of language spoken by the *baratero*. There are also significant cultural references to Spain and uses of language (slang) of the time.

THE TRANSCRIPT OF MANUAL DEL BARATERO

Scans of the original book are available online from university and literature digitisation projects. I have included this transcript as the full text is not readily available. My preference is to have the original language alongside the English, and include it this way for readers, so that they can continue to review, cross check, and gain better understanding of the writing in its original form and context. I have attempted to remain as faithful to the original printing as possible. Note that this transcript uses spelling and word forms that may no longer be correct in modern Spanish. I have also kept the page breaks from the original.

THE TRANSLATION

The transcription and my translation have been laid out side by side for ease of reference and review. As you read the translation, please understand that I have tried to minimise the interpretation in favour of keeping the flow, manner, and flavour of the original. Thus, the reader will find that sometimes the words and syntax do not strictly follow the rules of modern English. Some words, usually the names of specific techniques have been left in Spanish, identified in italics, and in most cases some attempt at explaining these words has been included in the glossary and notes. Words in [ ] are my inclusions to provide quick insight or clarification.

MANUAL
DEL
BARATERO,

ó

ARTE DE MANEJAR LA NAVAJA,
EL CUCHILLO Y LA TIJERA DE LOS JITANOS.

MADRID: 1849
IMPRENTA DE D. ALBERTO GOYA.

MANUAL OF THE BARATERO

or

THE ART OF HANDLING THE NAVAJA,
THE KNIFE AND THE SCISSORS OF THE JITANOS.

MADRID: 1849.
PRINTED BY D. ALBERTO GOYA

MANUAL

DEL

BARATERO,

ó

ARTE DE MANEJAR LA NAVAJA,

EL CUCHILLO Y LA TIJERA DE LOS JITANOS.

MADRID: 1849.

IMPRENTA DE D. ALBERTO GOYA.

PROLOGO

Quizá habrá algunos que al ver el presente Manual lo reciban malamente, suponiendo perjudicial su aparicion, por ser la navaja el arma propia de los barateros, de los tahúres y de otras ciertas jentes de vida airada, las cuales deberian mas bien ignorar que aprender unos preceptos que redundarian en daño suyo, y por consiguiente en el de la sociedad. A los que tal dijeren, podremos contestar manifestándoles que, cuando en esta sociedad hay ciertos males irremediables para los cuales no bastan los preceptos de la relijion, ni los tratados de la moral mas sublime, ni sirven las leyes, ni alcanzan nada las medidas mas eficazes; conviene adoptar un medio á fin de hacer que dichos males sean menos crueles, y es aleccionar a aquellos hombres honrados y pazificos que puedan verse acometidos inicuamente por los que hacen alarde de destreza en el manejo de las armas, y escudados con esta ventaja acuden el insulto y á la ofensa por la cosa ó palabra mas insigificante ó por puro placer de hacer daño.

PROLOGUE

Perhaps there will be some who upon seeing the present Manual will receive it badly, supposing its appearance to be harmful, because the *navaja* is the weapon of the *barateros*, of the *tahúres* and of other certain people of the criminal life [the underworld], those who would ignore rather than learn [from] precepts that would result in their harm, and consequently in that of society. To those who say such, we can reply by stating manifestly that, when in this society there are certain irremediable evils for which the precepts of religion are not enough, nor the treatises of the most sublime morality, nor do the laws serve, nor do the most effective measures achieve; it is advisable to adopt a means to make those said evils less cruel, and it [the *Manual*] is to instruct those honourable and peaceful men who may be iniquitously attacked by those who make a display of skill in the handling of weapons, and shielded with this advantage follow [up] the insult and the offense for the most insignificant thing or word or for the pure pleasure of doing harm.

Leyes represivas contra el duelo tiene la lejislacion española, tratando de estirpar esta bárbara costumbre que nos legaron los tiempos caballerescos, y en verdad que nada ha podido conseguirse: pues estamos viendo diariamente apelar á ese combate que llaman de honor á los hombres encargados precisamente de vijilar por el cumplimiento de las repetidas pragmáticas, órdenes y códigos que lo proiben.

No basta que haya personas intelijentes y virtuosas que se levanten contra los desafios, llamándolos el *recurso de los bribones y de los hombres inmorales*; y en vano se han formado en otros paises mas ilustrados que el nuestro asociaciones respetables á fin de acabar con ellos, empleando todos los recursos que puede dictar el amor mas acendrado á la humanidad.

El duelo continúa; y hemos visto *con escándalo* no hace mucho tiempo, que las leyes se desprecian por los mismos que las establecen.

"Guardaos, ha dicho Rousseau, hablando contra el duelo, de confundir el nombre sagrado del honor con esa preocupacion feroz que pone todas las virtudes en la punta de una espada, y que solo es propia para hacer valientes infames. ¿En qué consiste esta preocupacion? En la oplnlon mas estravagante y bárbara que entró jamás en el espíritu humano, á saber que los deberes de la sociedad se suplen con el valor;

The Spanish laws have repressive legislation against the duel, trying to stamp out this barbarous custom that is the legacy of knightly times, and in truth nothing has been achieved: for we see daily the appeal to this combat, the call of honour, to men precisely in charge of watching out for the compliance of those repeated pragmatics[9], orders and codes that prohibit it.

It is not enough that there are intelligent and virtuous people who rise up against the challenges [duels], calling them the recourse of crooked and immoral men; and in vain they formed in other countries, more enlightened than ours, respectable associations to the aim of finishing with them, using all the resources that are dictated by the most pure love of humanity.
The duel continues; and we have seen with scandal not so long ago, that the laws are despised by the same men that establish them.

"Beware, said Rousseau, speaking against the duel, of confusing the sacred name of honour with this fierce concern that puts all the virtues on the point of a sword, and that is only proper to make the brave infamous. What is this concern? In the most extravagant and barbaric opinion that ever entered the human spirit, to know that the duties of society are supplanted with valour [bravado];

que hombre no es picaro, bribon ne calumniador, y por el contrario es politico, cortés, bien educado y humano cuando sabe batirse; que la mentirá se trueca en verdad, en honradéz la perfidia, y se hace laudable la infidelidad en el momento que se sostienen con el acero en la mano; que una afrenta queda reparada siempre bien por medio de una estocada; y que nunca se comete una sinrazon con un hombre con tal que se le mate."

Véase aquí un poco de lo mucho que se ha dicho contra el desafio, y sin embargo de todo no faltan en nuestros días escritores que publiquen tratados apolojéticos defendiéndolo, sin cuidarse de que sus doctrinas estén en oposicion con las leyes. ¿Qué demuestra esto? la insuficiencia de dichas leyes, y el triunfo de las doctrinas de los duelistas.

Tolerado pues, el desafio, se hace necesaria la enseñanza del arte de manejar las armas para que sus efectos sean menos sensibles; ha habido una necesidad de instruir al débil para que sepa defenderse de las demasías del fuerte; y desde tiempos muy lejanos hay hombres que llevan el titulo pomposo de *Maestro mayor de los reinos*, otros que se dicen *Segundos tenientes*, y por último los simplemente nombrados *Maestros de armas*, los cuales llaman á la coleceion de sus preceptos *El nobilísimo arte de la esgrima*.

that man is not a scoundrel, rogue nor slanderer [liar], and on the contrary he is political, courteous, well educated and humane when he knows how to fight; that the lie will become truth, in honesty the treachery, and it makes laudable the infidelity in the moment they hold steel in their hands; that an affront is always repaired [well-remedied] by means of a thrust; and that you never commit an injustice to a man so long as you kill him."

See here a little of how much has been said against the challenge, and yet in our days there is no lack of writers who publish apologetic treatises defending it [duelling], without taking care that their doctrines are in opposition to the laws. What does this demonstrate? The insufficiency of said laws, and the triumph of the doctrines of the duellists.

Tolerated then, the challenge, it necessary to teach the art of handling weapons so that their effects are less noticeable; there has been a need to instruct the weak so they know to defend themselves against the excesses of the strong; and since very distant times there are men who carry the pompous title of Senior Master of the kingdom, others who are called Second Lieutenants, and finally the simply named Masters of Arms, which they call the collection of their precepts The Noble Art of Fencing.

Esos maestros de esgrima ó de destreza, como se llamaban en lo antiguo, establezen sus *palestras* aun en los sitios mas públicos, y dan en ellas sus lecciones, sin que la autoridad, protectora de la vida de lós ciudadanos, destruya esas cátedras de lás cuales no han de salir sinó verdaderos homicidas; y véase aquí una contradiccion entre una ley que proibe el desafio, y otra que autoriza ó da carta de ecsámen á los preceptors públicos de florete. ¿Qué otra cosa son esos *asaltos* dados aún por personas del secso femenino, sínó escuelas, cuyos maestros enseñan á alcanzar triunfos con sangre humana? ¿De qué hace alarde la llamada señorita Castellanos en sus sesiones de florete? de saber matar. ¿Por qué se permite la enseñanza del tiro de pistola? porque hay ocasiones en que conviene usarla en defensa propia.

Luego, si aun conociéndose que és un mal atróz el desafio hay que tolerarlo, y conviene que se enseñe el modo de batirse; si nadie se escandaliza ni se levanta contra un tratado de esgrima, ni contra sus preceptos, antes por el contrario estos forman parte de la buena educacion de las altas clases, y no es uno cumplido caballero si no sabe empuñar un florete ó dar sablazos; si todo esto sucede, no hallamos razon para que alguno mirase con repugnancia la enseñanza de la navaja, y mucho mas cuando nos proponemos dar preceptos á los hombres honra-

Those teachers of fencing or destreza, as they were called in history, establish their halls even in the most public places, and give in them their lessons, without the Authorities, protectors of the lives of the citizens, destroy those *cathedra*[10] from which will emerge nothing if not true murderers: and see here a contradiction between a law that prohibits the challenge, and another that authorises or gives letters of examination [rank] to the public preceptors of foil. What else are those assaults given even by persons of the feminine gender, save schools, whose masters teach to reach triumphs with [by] human blood? What does *señorita Castellanos*[11] boast about in her foil sessions? Of knowing how to kill. Why is it permitted to teach how to shoot a pistol? Because there are occasions when it is convenient to use it in self-defence.

Then, if even knowing that it is an atrocious evil the challenge must be tolerated, and it is advisable to teach the way to fight; If no one is scandalised or rises against a treatise of fencing, nor against its precepts, before on the contrary these form part of the good education of the upper classes, and a gentleman is not complete if he does not know how to wield a foil or give a sabre cut; If all this happens, we find no reason for anyone to look with disgust at the teaching of the *navaja*, and much more when we propose to give the precepts to honourable men

dos para que sepan usarla como arma defensiva. Es indudable que no serian tan temibles ciertas jentecillas de navaja si se supiesen parar sus golpes; y una prueba de ello es, que cuando dos personas se desafian al florete, como ambas lo sepan manejar, por lo regular la pelea no suele traer funestas consecuencias. La navaja es un arma usada jeneralmente en España por la clase trabajadora, y nos choca sobremanera esa aversion con que la miran los que pertenecen á clases mas elevadas. Aprendan pues á manejarla para ciertas ocasiones así como aprenden el uso de las demás armas, y conocerán la utilidad de nuestro Manual. Si se nos dice que es el arma con que los barateros imponen la ley en los garitos y sacan la contribucion forzosa á los jugadores, diremos tambien que lo es del hombre honrado y pazifico que se encuentra acometido por un ratero, por un truan, y que no tiene otro medio de defensa que ella y su corazon. La navaja en fin, es el arma propia, como ya hemos dicho, de la clase trabajadora, del arriero, del trajinero, del artesano, del marinero, y un instrumento tan indispensable que muchos no pueden estar sin él. En vista de esto, vamos á fijar aquí las reglas necesarias para su mejor manejo en esos casos que se llaman de *honra*.

Además, si hay quien escriba tratados especiales de esgrima y del tiro de todas las ar-

so they know how to use it as a defensive weapon. It is undoubtable that they would not be so fearsome of the *navaja* of certain rabble if they knew how to stop their blows; and a proof of this is, that when two people challenge to foil, as both know how to handle them, usually the fight does not bring fatal consequences. The *navaja* is a weapon used generally in Spain by the working class, and we are exceedingly shocked by that aversion with which those who belong to higher classes look at it. Learn then to handle it for certain occasions as well as you learn the use of those other weapons, and you will know the usefulness of our Manual. If we are told that it is the weapon with which the *barateros* impose the law in the gambling dens and forcefully take the contribution from the players, we will say also that it is for the honourable and peaceful man that finds himself attacked by a thief, by a vagabond, and has no other means of defence than her [the *navaja*] and his heart. The *navaja* in the end, is the proper weapon, as we have already said, of the working class, of the mule driver, of the *trajinero*, of the craftsman, of the sailor, and an instrument so indispensable that many can not be without it. In view of this, we are going to set here the necessary rules for its better handling in those cases that are called for *honour*.

In addition, as there is someone who writes special treaties for fencing and fighting of all weapons

—mas para los caballeros, para los nobles, para los hombres de guante blanco y paletó, nosotros escribimos, para el pueblo, para los hombres del pueblo, para esos de manos endurecidas y callosas á quienes los señores llaman *la canalla*, y sin la cual valdrian bien poco; y escribimos para los hombres del pueblo, porque estos tienen tambien sus desafios, casi siempre mas repentinos, mas bruscos, sin padrinos ni testigos, ni otras zarandajas ni pamemas usadas en los duelos aristocráticos y de jente llamada decente.

Por último, escribimos tambien este Manual por si de nuestros conocimientos quieren valerse esos espadachines de profesíon, los cuales aunque perfumados y vestidos de ricos trajes, están muy lejos de tener mejor conducta y moralidad que los hombres de chaqueta y palo, y son muchas vezes mas dignos de castigo que los héroes de los garitos, entre quienes no es estraño encontrar rasgos particulares que están en contradiccion con su vida truanesca y peleadora.

M. d. R.

for the gentlemen, for the nobles, for the men in white gloves and fancy coats, we write, for the people, for the men of the towns, for those with hardened and callused hands whom the lords [gentlemen] call the *la canalla* [scoundrels], and without whom they would be worth very little; and we write for the men of the town, because they also have their challenges, almost always more sudden, more abrupt, without sponsors or witnesses, or other nonsense nor trivial things used in aristocratic duels and so-called decent people.

Finally, we also write this Manual in case use those professional swordsmen want our knowledge, those who although perfumed and dressed in rich costumes, are far from having better conduct and morality than the men of jacket and stick, and they are much of the time more worthy of punishment than the heroes of the gambling dens, among whom it is not uncommon to find particular qualities in contradiction to their vagrant and combative life.

M. d. R.

INSTRUCCION

PARA MANEJAR LA NAVAJA.

La instruccion para manejar la navaja se divide en cuatro partes.

La primera comprende el mecanismo del arma y las diferentes posiciones.

En la segunda se analizan las guardias, y se esplica el modo de acometer al contrario, dando una lijera idea de las varia suertes que se ejecuta, y de las tretas.

En la tercera se ensena el modo de manejar el cuchillo (1).

Últimamente, en la cuarta se ensena el manejo des las Tijeras entre los jitanos.

La primera parte se divide en once lecciones, la segunda en doce, la tercera en seis, y la cuarta en dos, del modo siguiente.

PRIMERA PARTE.

Leccion primera ...	De la navaja.
Leccion segunda ...	Sus nombres mas usuales.
Leccion tercera ...	Posiciones ó plantas.
Leccion cuarta ...	Modos de acometer y defenderse.
Leccion quinta ...	Del terreno.

(1) Bajo el epigrafe de "*Instruccion para manejar la navaja*" comprendemos aqui el manejo del cuchillo y las Tijeras, á fin de que encuentren mayor claridad los lectores.

INSTRUCTION

TO WIELD THE NAVAJA.

The instruction to wield the *navaja* is divided into four parts.

The first comprises the mechanism of the weapon and the different positions.

In the second it analyses the guards, and explains the way to attack the opponent, giving a slight idea of various techniques that are executed, and of the tricks.

In the third it teaches the way to handle the knife (1).

Finally, in the fourth it teaches the handling of the *Tijeras* [scissors] among the *jitanos*.

The first part is divided into eleven lessons, the second in twelve, the third in six, and the fourth in two, as follows.

FIRST PART.

First lesson …	Of the *navaja*.
Second lesson …	Their most usual names.
Third lesson …	Positions or stances.
Fourth lesson …	Methods of attack and defence.
Fifth lesson …	Of the *terreno* [terrain].

(1) Under the epigraph of "*Instruction to wield the navaja*" we understand here the handling of the knife and the scissors, so that the readers may find more clarity.

Leccion sesta ...	De los jiros y modos de hacerlos.
Leccion setima...	De los contrajiros.
Leccion octava...	Cambios.
Leccion novena...	De los golpes.
Leccion decima...	De los quites y huidas.
Leccion undecimal...	De los recursos.

SEGUNDA PARTE.

DE LAS VARIAS SUERTES QUE SE EJECUTAS AL JUGAR LA NAVAJA

Leccion primera...	Guardias.
Leccion segunda...	Golpes de frente.
Leccion tercera...	Golpes de costado.
Leccion cuarta...	Corridas.
Leccion quinta...	Molinete.
Leccion sesta...	Lanzar la navaja.
Leccion setima...	Pases de mano y de sombrero.
Leccion octava...	Recortes.
Leccion novena...	Suerte de la culebra.
Leccion decima...	Engaños.
Leccion undecimal..	Tretas.

TERCERA PARTE.

Leccion primera...	Del cuchillo.
Leccion segunda....	Posiciones.
Leccion tercera...	Golpes, modo de lanzar el puñal.
Leccion cuarta...	Quites y huidas.
Leccion quinta...	Recursos y tretas.
Leccion sesta...	Defensas del cuchillo ó puñal.

CUARTA PARTE.

Leccion primera...	Del las tijeras.
Leccion segunda...	Modo de manejarlas entre los jitanos.

Sixth Lesson…	Of the *jiros* and ways of doing them.
Seventh lesson…	Of the *contrajiros*.
Eighth lesson…	Cambios [Changes]
Ninth Lesson…	Of the blows.
Tenth lesson…	Of the retreats and escapes [voids].
Eleventh lesson…	Of the responses.

SECOND PART.
OF THE VARIOUS TECHNIQUES THAT ARE EXECUTED WHEN PLAYING THE NAVAJA

First lesson…	Guards.
Second lesson…	Blows on the front.
Third lesson…	Blows on the side.
Fourth lesson…	*Corridas* [Runs].
Fifth lesson…	Wheel.
Sixth lesson…	Throwing the *navaja*.
Seventh lesson…	Passes of the hand and hat.
Eighth lesson…	Cutaways
Ninth lesson…	Technique of the snake.
Tenth Lesson…	Deceptions.
Eleventh lesson…	Tricks.

THIRD PART.

First lesson…	Of the knife.
Second lesson…	Positions.
Third lesson…	Blows, way to throw the thrust.
Fourth lesson…	Retreats and escapes.
Fifth lesson…	Responses [recourses] and tricks.
Sixth lesson…	Defences of the knife or *puñal*.

FOURTH PART.

First lesson…	Of the scissors.
Second lesson…	Ways to handle them among the *jitanos*.

INSTRUCCION DE LA NAVAJA.

PARTE PRIMERA.

LECCION PRIMERA.

DE LA NAVAJA.

Siendo la navaja un arma demasiado conocida en nuestro pais, no cansaremos á nuestros lectores con una minuciosa esplicacíon de su sencillo mecanismo. Bastará saber que las hay de diferentes tamanos, y que no todas son á propósito para nuestro objeto.

En Espana hay varios pueblos notables por la buena calidad y temple que dan á las hojas de las navajas, siendo de admirar el agudo filo en que rematan y que no se quiebra ni se tuerze después de haber atravesado dos pesos duros ó una tabla del grueso de dos pulgadas. Albacete, Santa Cruz de Mudela, Guadij, Solana, Mora, Bonilla, Valencia, Sevilla, Jaen y otros muchos puntos tienen maestros de herrería, de cuyas manos salen obras mejor acabadas en ese jénero

INSTRUCTION OF THE NAVAJA.

FIRST PART.

FIRST LESSON.//
OF THE NAVAJA.

The knife being a weapon too well known in our country, we will not tire our readers with a meticulous explanation of its simple mechanism. It will be enough to know that they are of different sizes, and that not all are intended for our purpose.

In Spain there are several notable towns for the good quality and temper that they give to the blades of the *navaja*, being to admire the sharp edge with which they are finished and that do not break or twist after having gone through two hard coins or a table two inches thick. Albacete, Santa Cruz de Mudela, Guadij, Solana, Mora, Bonilla, Valencia, Seville, Jaen and many other places have masters of blacksmithing, from whose hands come works better finished in that style

que las que puede producir el estranjero, y que recomendamos á los aficionados. Pero como la figura de la navaja no siempre es adecuada para el uso que le habremos de dar en el curso de nuestra esplicacion, diremos que la hoja deberá tener á lo mas un palmo de lonjitud, y estar perfectamente segura entre las cachas, prefiriéndose la navaja de muelle á otra cualquiera.

La figura de la hoja es de gran interés, pues no con cualquiera puede arriesgarse el diestro á tirar todo golpe indistintamente. Asi, pues, será la elejida de mucha panza ácia el estremo de la punta, teniendo de tres á cuatro dedos de latitud ó sea de anchura, y con punta algo prolongada, para dar los *floretazos*; todo segun indica la presente figura.

[Image – navaja]

LECCION SEGUNDA.
DE LOS NOMBRES QUE RECIBE LA NAVAJA.

La navaja recibe varios nombres entre las personas que la manejan. Nosotros no pondremos aqui todos, y si solamente los que se encuentran mas en uso, pues cada provincial le suele dar uno.

En Andalucia la llaman *la mojosa*, *la chaira*, *la tea*, y en Sevilla á las de mucha lonjitud *las*

than those that foreigners can produce, and that we recommend to the aficionados. Yet as the figure of the *navaja* is not always adequate for the use that we will give in the course of our explanation, we will say that the blade must have over one palm of length, and be perfectly secure between the handle, preferring the switch blade to any other.

The figure of the blade is of great interest, since the *diestro* can not risk with any [blade] to throw every blow equally[12]. So, then, choose one of much belly towards the end of the point, having three to four fingers of breadth or width, and with a somewhat prolonged point, to give the *floretazos*; all just as shown in the present figure.

[Image – *navaja*]

SECOND LESSON.
OF THE NAMES THAT THE NAVAJA RECEIVES.

The *navaja* receives several names among the people who handle them. We will not put all here, and only those that are found more in use, because each province usually gives one to use.

In Andalusia they call it the *mojosa*, the *chaira*, the *tea*, and in Seville the ones of great length *those*

del Santólio; pero en los presidios y cárceles, entre los barateros de Madrid y otros puntos es conocida con los nombres de *corte, herramienta, pincho, hierro, abanico, alfiler* y algun otro. En nuestras lecciones la llamaremos con el jeneral de navaja.

LECCION TERCERA.
DE LAS POSICIONES O PLANTAS.

El diestro en el manejo de la navaja tiene su primera posicion ó planta, del mismo modo que en el de la espada y sable, que se llama guardia. Despues de tomar la navaja con cualquiera de las manos colocando el dedo pulgar sobre el primer tercio de la hoja, cuyo corte deberá caer ácia la parte de adentro, se plantará en guardia á respectable distancia de su contrario, mas bien lejos que cerca, con la mano desocupada pegada al cuerpo por la parte de la cintura y delantera del vientra, y en disposicion de recojer la navaja cuando se quiera hacer un *cambio*, los pies y piernas los colocará á igual distancia del contrario, un poco abiertas, y de modo que le dé todo el cuerpo de frente, como se ve en la presente figura y de

[Image - planta]

of the *Santólio*; but in the garrisons and prisons, among the *barateros* of Madrid and other places it is known by the names of cutter, tool, skewer, iron, fan, pin and some others. In our lessons we will call it by the general name of *navaja*.

THIRD LESSON.

OF POSITIONS OR STANCES[13]

Those skilled in handling the knife have their first position or stance, in the same way as in the sword and sabre, which is called a guard. After taking the knife with either of the hands place the thumb on the first third of the blade, whose edge should fall to the inside, stand in guard at respectable distance from the opponent, better far than close, with the unoccupied hand held against the body at the waist and in front of the belly, and in disposition to bring up to the knife when you want to make an exchange [of hands], place the feet and legs at an equal distance from the opponent, a little open, and of a manner that all of the body is to the front, as is seen in the present figure and

[Image - stance]

ningun modo de costado; á no ser que en alguna de las manos se use de sombrero, capa, chaqueta ó manta, en cuyo caso deberá colocarse con la pierna compañera del brazo en que este el sombrero ó capa, ácia adelante y de la manera que marca la figures que se halla en la leccion octava, de los *Cambios*.

Al caer en guardia se tendrá cuidado de recojer el vientre todo lo possible, para cuyo efecto habrá que encorvarse un poco, sin que por eso se saque demasiado la cara, pues es recibiria un golpe en ella, y fuera muy vergonzoso. La vista estará siempre fija en la del contrario; de tal suerte que no se variará de modo alguno, aunque éste trate de obligar á ello con engaños, palabras ó jestos; pues hay que advertir que el tirar bien a la navaja, consiste esencialmente en la lijereza de ojos y de pies, como iremos viendo en adelante.

LECCION CUARTA.
MODOS DE ACOMETER Y DEFENDERSE.

Despues que los combatientes se hallan colocados en su guardia, cuidara cada uno de no acometer de pronto a su contrario, y su esperar ser acometido por el para recibirle como es debido y conocer se destreza.

Para la intelijencia del mejor modo de atacar y defenderse, vamos a esplicar en las lecciones sucesivas lo que se entiende por *terreno*, *jiros*, *contrajiros* y *cambios*, palabras cuyo significado y conocimiento nos es indispensable.

of no manner sideways; unless in the hands is used a hat, coat, jacket or blanket, in which case it should be placed with the leg matching the arm in which is the hat or cape, towards the front and in the manner marked by the figure found in the eighth lesson, of the *Cambios*.

When you fall into guard you have to be careful to withdraw the belly as much as possible, for which effect you will have to stoop a little, without which you put your face out too much, it will receive a blow, and is very shameful. The gaze will always be fixed on the opponent; in such a way that it will not waver in any way, even if they try to force it with tricks, words or gestures; it is necessary to advise that wielding the *navaja* well, consists essentially in the lightness [agility] of eyes and feet, as we will see from now on.

FOURTH LESSON.
MODES OF ATTACK AND DEFENCE.

After the combatants are positioned in their guards, each one should take care not to attack his opponent quickly, yet wait to be attacked by him to receive him as is proper and to get to know his skill[14].

For the knowledge of the best way to attack and defend, we are going to explain in the successive lessons what is understood by *terreno*, *jiros*, *contrajiros* and *cambios*, words whose significance and knowledge is indispensable to us.

LECCION QUINTA.

DEL TERRENO.

Llámase *terreno* el espacio comprendido en toda la estension del brazo y la navaja del diestro, dentro del cual solamente puede herir a su adversario.

Por lo tanto habrá dos *terrenos*, uno el terreno *propio*, y otro el terreno contrario.

LECCION SESTA.

JIROS Y MODO DE HACERLOS.

En los *jiros* estriba la mayor dificultad de este arte, necesitandose para hacerlos bien una admirable velozidad, que se adquiere con el mucho ejercicio.

Colocados los combatientes, uno enfrente de otro dejando entre sus *terrenos* el espacio de otro procsimamente, hará el diestro el *jiro* para arrojarse sobre el contrario y alcanzar á herirle, adelantando insensiblemente ó de pronto uno de los pies y jirando el cuerpo de repente sobre su punta.

Cuando estan en guardia los tiradores, no pueden llegarse á herir sin aprocsimarse, y el medio mas rapido y seguro de ejecutarlo es con un jiro que se podra duplicar y triplicar, si el que los recibe huye el bulto.

Los jiros se hacen por el lado derecho y por el lado izquierdo.

Para hacerlos por el lado derecho, y por consiguiente para alcanzar al contrario por su costado izquierdo, será preciso avanzar con el pie izquierdo y jirar sobre él velozmente; hecho

FIFTH LESSON.

OF THE TERRENO [TERRAIN].

All the space comprised by the extension of the arm and *navaja* of the *diestro* is called the *terreno*, only within which can he hurt his adversary.

Therefore there will be two *terreno*, one's own terreno, and the other the opponent's terreno.

SIXTH LESSON.

JIROS AND HOW TO DO THEM.

In the *jiros* lay the greatest difficulty of this art, admirable speed is necessary to do them well, that is acquired with much practice.

The combatants are positioned, one in front of the other leaving between their *terreno* the space of another, the *diestro* will make the *jiro* to throw himself upon the opponent and reach to wound him, imperceptibly or quickly advancing one of the feet and suddenly turning the body on its point [ball of the foot].

When the *tiradores* are on guard, they can not be hurt without approaching each other, and the fastest and safest way to execute it is with a *jiro* that can be doubled and tripled, if the receiver escapes the space.

Jiros are made on the right side and on the left side.

For making them on the right side, and therefore to reach the opponent on the left side, it will be necessary to advance with the left foot and to turn fast upon it;

lo cual, si aquel no hace un *contrajiro* ó una *huida*, será herido indudablamente.

Para hacerlos por el lado izquierdo, se jira sobre el pie derecho, teniendo cuidado de colocar en el mismo instante la navaja en la mano izquierdo con la que se ha de dar el *golpe*; si no es que ya estuviere anteriormente en dicha mano.

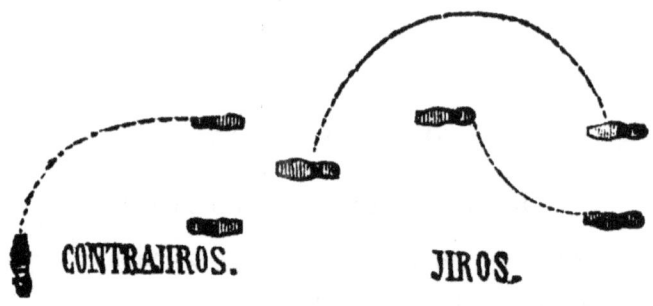

LECCION SETIMA.
DE LOS CONTRAJIROS.

Los contrajiros no son otra cosa que los mismos jiros que hace el diestro que es acometido con uno de ellos, cuidando que sean al revés del que le hacen; es decir, si le viene un jiro por el lado derecho, jira sobre el pie del mismo lado, y huye el costado acometido ácia la parte de atrás, librándose así del golpe y pudiendo *atracar* á su contrario jeneralmente por la parte posterior del pecho. El jiro es siempre avanzando, el contrajiro retrocediendo. De manera que un jiro tirado es destruido con un contrajiro, el cual es á su vez destruido con un segundo jiro, y este con un segundo contrajiro, y así sucesivamente; es la suerte mas bonita y de major perspectíva que presenta el manejo de la navaja. Véase el grabado anterior.

that done, if he does not make a *contrajiro* or an escape, he will undoubtedly be wounded.

For making them [*jiros*] to the left side, the turn is on the right foot, taking care to place at the same instant the *navaja* in the left hand with which the blow has to be given; if it was not already previously in that hand.

[Image – *jiros* and *contrajiros*]

SEVENTH LESSON.

OF THE CONTRAJIROS [COUNTER JIROS].

The *contrajiros* are nothing other than the same *jiros* made by the *diestro* who is attacked with one of them, taking care to be the reverse of what they [opponent] do to him, that is to say, if a *jiro* comes from the right side, he turns [*contrajiro*] on the foot of the same side, and the side attacked escapes behind, thus he becomes free from the blow and is able to attack his opponent generally to the back part of the chest. The *jiro* is always advancing, the *contrajiro* moving back. The manner in which a *jiro* is destroyed is with a *contrajiro*, which is in turn destroyed with a second *jiro*, and this with a second *contrajiro*, and so on; It is the most beautiful and best perspective to introduce the handling of the *navaja*. See the previous engraving.

LECCION OCTAVA.

CAMBIOS.

De los varios modos que hay de tirar á la navaja, es el mejor y mas seguro el que se verifica con ambas manos, es decir, pudiendo usar de cualquiera de ellas para su manejo, aunque algunos colocan en uno de los brazos la capa, manta Ó chaqueta, ó bien el sombrero en la mano. Pero además de tener muy pocas ventajas esta manera de tirar, trae consigo muchas desventajas que deben tomarse en consideracion. Efectivamente, si atendemos á la facilidad con que puede variarse la vista del contrario con el sombrero en la mano, y al obstáculo que este presenta, á manera de escudo, á los golpes que vienen al diestro, seguramente que debiéramos adoptar como mas á propósito esta antigua costumbre de ponerse en guardia ó de tirar á la navaja; mas si nos detenemos á ecsaminar las muchas contras y hasta perjuicios que se siguen de no poder ejecutar los cambios ni acometer sino es por el lado de la mano armada, al mismo tiempo que la esposicion y riesgo en que se encuentra el diestro ó tirador en la guardia que ecsije esta manera de tírar, como representa esta figura, deduciremos sin duda alguna que el me-

[Image – sombrero en la mano]

EIGHTH LESSON.

CHANGES.

Of the several ways that there are to wield the *navaja*, It is best and safest to be used with both hands, that is to say, being able to use either of them [hands] for its handling, although some place onto one of the arms the coat, blanket or jacket, or the hat in the hand. But besides this manner of wielding having a few advantages, it brings with it many disadvantages that must be taken into consideration. Indeed, if we look at the ease with which the view of the opponent can be changed [obscured] with the hat in the hand, and the obstacle that this presents, a way of shielding, those blows that come to the *diestro*, surely we should adopt purposefully this old habit of getting in guard or wielding the *navaja*; but if we stop to study the many disadvantages and even harms that follow from not being able to execute those *cambios* nor attack except from the side of the armed hand, at the same time the position and risk which the *diestro* or *tirador* is in from the guard that this way of fighting demands, as this figure represents, we will deduce without doubt that the

[Image – hat in the hand]

-dio mas seguro y de mas recursos es usando de ambas manos para el combate, ó sea una mano armada y la otra desarmada y libre, pero en disposicion de poderse armar tomando la navaja de la otra mano que quedará á su vez desarmada.

Es tal la velozidad que se necesita en esta suerte, que se llama *cambio*, que puestos en combate los dos tiradores, apenas la vista del uno puede penetrar en qué mano del otro se halla la navaja; y de aquí el no arriesgarse á acometer sinó con una lijereza mayor, que la que en igualdad de circunstancias se necesitaria para la otra manera de tirar que arriba hemos refutado.

No entiendan por eso nuestros lectores que reprobamos en todas ocasiones el que el diestro ocupe una mano con el sombrero; por el contrario lo admitimos en algunos casos, considerando que es mas bien una suerte especial del arte, que una escuela aislada, sin embargo de ser tenida por tal entre algunos.

Para usar de esa suerte durante el combate, cuidará el diestro de no quitarse el sombrero de la cabeza y de que no caiga al suelo en las varias corridas y huidas que haga, con el objeto de apoderarse en ocasiones de él y colocarle en la mano desarmada, ó para arrojarle á los ojos del contrario ó finjirlo solamente, como mas adelante se dirá. Advertiremos de paso, que es de gran utilidad al diestro llevar faja á la cintura, ya para cubrir una parte del vientre y los vacíos, y resistir de ese modo algun tanto por lo menos los *desjarretazos* y *viajes*, ya para ejecutar varias *tretas* con ella, y que en su respective lugar esplicaremos.

Cuando el diestro es citado ó provocado á re-

method most secure and with more responses is using both hands for combat, or that is one hand armed and the other unarmed and free, but in a position to be able to arm itself by taking the knife of the other hand that will in turn become unarmed.

Such is the speed that is necessary in this technique, which is called the *cambio*, that when done in the combat between two *tiradores*, the vision of one is hardly able to fathom in which hand of the other is the *navaja*; and from here he will not risk to attack without a greater agility, that which in equal circumstances would be needed for the other manner of wielding that we have refuted above.

Our readers, do not think that we condemn on all occasions that the *diestro* occupy one hand with the hat; on the contrary we admit in some cases, considering that it is rather a special type of art, an isolated school, nevertheless to be considered as such among some.

To benefit from this technique during the fight, the *diestro* will take care not to remove the hat from his head and that it does not fall to the ground in the various *corridas* and *huidas* that are made, with the object of seizing it on occasion and placing it in his unarmed hand, or to throw it at the eyes of the opponent or to just pretend, as it will be said later. We advise in passing, that it is of great utility to the *diestro* to wear a sash at the waist, and to cover a part of the belly and the gaps, and to resist in some way at least the *desjarretazos* and *viajes*[15], and to execute several tricks with it, and that will be explained in its respective place.

When the *diestro* is called or provoked

-nir tendrá buen cuidado, si lleva capa, de arrojarla en sitio donde no pueda incomodarle enredándose entre sus pies; y de ningun modo reñírá con ella colocada sobre los hombros, pues le estorbaria muchisimo en sus movimientos, si bien le libertaria muchas vezes de ser herido; pero aconsejamos á los peleadores que abandonen siempre la capa.

La capa se puede abandonar con prontitud y de manera que no trabe las piernas del diestro. Esta suerte consiste en hacer un pequeño encojimiento de hombros, al mismo tiempo que un sacudimiento leve con la parte media de los brazos; y la capa queda tendida en tierra en forma de media luna ó abanico, en cuyo centro se encuentra colocado el tirador. Este modo de líbertarse de la capa sin riesgo de que se envuelvan los pies del diestro, tiene por objeto el no perder de vista al contrario, lo cual sucedería ciertamente si volviera la cabeza, como tendría que hacerlo para lanzar la capa fuera de su terreno; en cuyo caso se vería espuesto á ser acometido por su contrario aun antes que pudiera pestañear; debiéndose advertir que, por desgracia, no todos los que usan y manejan la navaja, tienen la jenerosidad y buena intención que fueran de desear. Hacemos esta advertencia porque, como indicamos en el prólogo, no es la aficion que podamos tener al arte de tirar á la navaja y el deseo de jeneralizar su enseñanza, lo que nos mueve á escribir este Manual; es solamente el que tenemos de que los ignorantes de su manejo, se pongan al corriente de las reglas para cuando se vieren acometidos por los que abusan de él, del mismo modo que abusarian de cualquier clase de arma. Queremos

to fight take good care, if a cape is worn, to throw it where it can not bother him by getting entangled between his feet; and in no way fight with it placed on the shoulders, because it would impede him a lot in his movements, even if many times it keeps him from being hurt; but we advise the fighter to always abandon the cape.

The cape can be removed with speed and in a manner that does not trip the legs of the *diestro*. This technique consists of making a small shrug of the shoulders, at the same time as a slight shaking off with the middle part of the arms; and the cape is lying on the ground in the form of a half moon or fan, in whose center is placed the *tiradore*. This way of freeing oneself of the cape without risk of wrapping the feet of the *diestro*, the objective is to not lose sight of the opponent, which would certainly happen if he turned his head, as he would have to do to throw the cape on the ground; in which case he would be exposed to attack from his opponent before he could even blink; it must be noted that, disgracefully, not all those who use and wield the knife, have the generosity and good intention that would be desired. We make this warning because, as indicated in the prologue, it is not the affection we have for the art of striking with the *navaja* and the desire to generalise its teaching, which moves us to write this *Manual*; it is only for those that are ignorant of their handling, to be aware of the common rules for when they find themselves attacked by those who abuse them, in the same way that they would abuse any kind of weapon. We want to

destruir toda preocupacion, poniendo de manifiesto y al alcance de todas las personas, las diferentes suertes del arte y los medios, algunas vezes reprobados y de mal jenero, de que se valen los tiradores para reñir con los que no saben tomar la navaja en la mano. Con la lectura de esta *Instruccion* y una poca de práctica que fácilmente se adquiere, podrá cualquier almibarado señorito defenderse cuando menos del ataque mas brusco de un baratero.

LECCION NOVENA.
DE LOS GOLPES.

Colocados los tiradores uno enfrente de otro y con las navajas en mano, tratará cada uno de herir á su contrario, ó lo que es lo mismo, comenzarán á obrar las manos ó sean los *hierros*, con la ayuda de los movimientos de pies, que es lo mas esencial para dar los *golpes*.

Varias son las clases de *golpes* que pueden resultar de las diferentes posiciones y suertes que se ejecutan al tirar á la navaja; y reciben distinta denominacion segun la manera y sitio en que se dan, aunque todos están comprendidos bajo la jeneral de *golpes* ó *puñaladas*.

Ante todo diremos que el cuerpo del diestro tiene dos partes que se llaman la *parte alta* y la *parte baja*.

Por *parte alta* se entiende todo el medio cuerpo comprendido desde la cintura hasta la frente inclusive.

Por *parte baja* se entiende todo el medio cuerpo comprendido desde la cintura basta los

destroy all preoccupation, putting it clearly and within the reach of all people, the different types of the art and means, sometimes condemned and of bad character, that the *tiradores* make use of to quarrel with those who do not know how to take the *navaja* in hand. With the reading of this Instruction and a little practice that is easily acquired, any sugary rich kid[16] can at least defend himself from the most abrupt attack of a *baratero*.

NINTH LESSON.
OF THE BLOWS.

The *tiradores* are placed one in front of the other and with their *navaja* in hand, each one trying to wound their opponent, or like wise, they will begin to work their hands or their *hierros*, with the help of the movement of their feet, which is the most essential to give their blows.

Several are the kinds of blows that can result from the different positions and techniques that are executed when striking with the *navaja*; and they receive a different denomination according to the manner and place in which they are given, although all are included under the general [category] of blows or stabs.

Before anything we say that the body of the *diestro* has two parts that are called the upper part and the lower part.

The upper part means all the half body comprised from the waist to the forehead inclusive.

The lower part means all the entire half body from the waist including to the

pies. De manera que los golpes serán *altos* ó *bajos* segun que dén en la parte alta ó en la parte bajas.

Si la *puñala* ó *moja*, como dicen los jitanos, se da en cualquier punto de la estensíon del vientre, se dice á esta suerte *atracar*, y al *golpe* se le llama *viaje*; así suele decirse entre los barateros "*vamos á echar un viaje*" por "*vamos a reñir ó á darnos una puñalada.*" Cuando uno de los tiradores se arroja demasiado sobre el otro, este puede muy fácilmente herirle solo con estirar velozmente el brazo y presentarle la punta de la navaja en la parte alta las mas vezes, cuyo golpe recibe el nombre de *floretazo*, y ninguno mas adecuado por la semejanza que guarda con la estocada que se dá con el florete en igual círcunstancla, como se ve en las siguientes figuras.

[Image – floretazos]

No siempre el *floretazo* se dá en la parte alta, pues hay una suerte, que ocupa el primer lugar entre las mas seguras y de écsito mortal, que re-

feet. From the manner that the blows will be high or low according to whether they are given in the upper part or in the lower part.

If the *puñala* or *moja*, as the *jitanos* say, is given in any point of the belly, this technique is called *atracar* [to get stuck], and the blow is called *viaje*; when it is said among the *barateros* "*we are going to take a trip*" means "*we are going to quarrel or give each other a stab.*"

When one of the *tiradores* throws himself too much upon the other, he can very easily be hurt most times with just a quick stretch of the arm and presenting the point of the *navaja* to his upper part, which blow receives the name of *floretazo*, and none more appropriate because of the resemblance to that guard with the stab that is given with the foil in the same circumstances, as seen in the following figures.

[Image - *floretazos*]

The *floretazos* is not always given in the upper part, because there is a technique, which occupies the first place among the safest and of the deadly success, that

-quiere ese mismo golpe en el centro de la *parte baja*; -el modo de hacerla se dirá oportunamente.

El *jabeque ó chirlo* es el golpe dado en la cara, el cual imprime en ella un sello de ignominia para los barateros; pues en efecto, de todos los golpes que en riña puede el diestro recibir, ninguno hay que con mas verdad manifieste su poca destreza, y revele el desprecio con que le ha tratado su contrario.

A la accion de herir en la cara se le llama *enfilar*.

El golpe dado en la parte alta y detrás de los vacíos por encima de las costillas, tiene por nombre *desjarretazo*; y es uno de los que prueban la habilidad del que le tira, abriendo algunas vezes con una ancha herida, la columna vertebral, llamada vulgarmente espinazo. Es mortal, y se da jeneralmente en los *jiros*.

Se entiende por *plumada*, el golpe ó puñalada tirado de derecha á izquierda describiendo jeneralmente una curva.

Llámase *revés*, el golpe lirado con la mano vuelta ácia fuera y de izquierda á derecha.

La *plumada* y el revés segun van esplicados se entenderán tirados con la mano derecha; pues si lo fueren con la mano izquierda, la *plumada* será de izquierda á derecha, y el *revés* da derecha á izquierda.

LECCION DECIMA.

QUITES, HUIDAS.

Ya habrán conocido nuestros lectores que el arte de tirar á la navaja no está fundado en el

requires that same blow in the center of the lower part; -the way of doing it will be told opportunely.

The *jabeque* or *chirlo* is the blow given in the face, which imprints upon it a stamp of ignominy for the *barateros*; for in effect, of all the blows that the *diestro* can receive, there is none that is more truthful to declare his lack of skill, and reveal the contempt with which he has treated his opponent.

The action of wounding in the face is called *enfilar*.

The blow given in the upper part and behind the gaps above the ribs, it has the name *desjarretazo*; and it is one of those that test the ability of the one who strikes, opening some times with a wide wound, the spine, vulgarly called *espinazo*. It is deadly, and usually given in the *jiros*.

It is understood by *plumada*, the blow or stab struck from right to left, generally describing a curve.

Called *reves*, the blow struck with the hand turned outwards and from left to right.

The *plumada* and the *reves* as just explained are understood to be struck with the right hand; for if they are with the left hand, the *plumada* will be from left to right, and the *reves* given right to left.

TENTH LESSON.

RETREATS, ESCAPES.

Our readers will already know, that the art of striking with the knife is not founded

solo capricho de algunos presidiarios ó jentes de mal vivir, y que está por el contrario, sujeto a reglas y principios tan esactos como los de la esgrima y el sable. Cuando lleguemos á hablar de algunas de las *tretas* que se usan en el manejo de la navaja, daremos la razón á los mas encarnizados detractores de esta arma, en lo que toca á aquellas, por ser su mayor parte nacida de la mas descuidada educacion y de los mas innobles sentimientos; pero hasta entonces, y prescindiendo de hechos que reprueban los hombres que se tienen en algo, sea de la clase que quiera, sostendremos que el arte de tirar á la navaja merece ser considerado del mismo modo que el de todas las otras armas.

Esplicados ya los medios de acometer, y las varias suertes de *golpes* mas dignas de atencion, vamos a dar ahora la esplicacion de los *quites* que están en práctica para la defensa; parte muy esencial en todo manejo de arma blanca, pues sin ella seria nulo y de ningun valor cuanto se dijera relativo al modo de ofender.

Se cree por muchos que el medio mas seguro de tirar á la navaja consiste en tener el cuerpo contínuamente en movimiento, suponiendo al diestro siempre brincando y siempre corriendo. Y nada hay seguramente con menos visos de verazidad: el diestro riñe con mucha calma y serenidad, y si bien salta grandes espacios y obra con prodijiosa líjereza, es cierto que lo ejecuta en ocasiones dadas y con muchísima oportunidad, moviéndose á vezes sin salir de un círculo de tres pies.

La serenidad hace al diestro ser oportono en los movimientos, y ésta solo se adquiere con el mucho ejercicio; de tal suerte, que llega á acos-

only on the caprice of some convicts or people of disrepute, and that to the contrary, subject to rules and principles as exact as those of fencing and the sabre. When we come to speak of some of the tricks that are used in the handling of the *navaja*, we will give the reason to the most fierce detractors of this weapon, as far as they [tricks] are concerned, for being the greater part born of the most neglected education and of the most ignoble sentiments; but until then, and regardless of the fact that some men disapprove, whatever their class, we maintain that the art of striking with the *navaja* deserves to be considered in the same way as all other weapons.

Having already explained the means of attacking, and the various types of blows more worthy of attention, we are going to now give the explanation of the *quites* that are in practice for the defence; a very essential part in all handling of *arma blanca*, because without it, it [the art of the *navaja*] would be null and void and of no value when it is discussed relative to the way of offending.

It is believed by many that the safest way to strike with the *navaja* consists in having the body continually in movement, supposing the *diestro* always jumping and always running [making the *corrida*]. And there is surely nothing less reflective of truth: the *diestro* quarrels with great calmness and serenity, and although he can jump large distances and works with prodigious agility, it is true that can he do so on given occasions and with great opportunities, moving at times without leaving a circle of three feet.

This serenity makes the *diestro* to be opportune in his movements, and this is only acquired with a lot of practice; of such ways, that become

-tumbrarse la vista á medir las distancias, y espera con tranquilidad y sin asustarse el golpe que le tira el contrario, cuando conoce que le ha de faltar una ó media pulgada para que alcance al cuerpo.

Si el golpe viene algo entrado en el terreno del diestro, se librará de él con encojer la parte del cuerpo amagada, y sin necesidad de huir ó brincar. Pero si la accion del contrario es para el diestro desconocida por su velozidad, ó el golpe que le tira se ha entrado hasta el centro del terreno, le esquivará con la huida brincando ácia atrás ó ácia un lado, á distancia suficiente para no ser alcanzado, y si pudiere ser, para alcanzar al que acomete; teniendo sumo cuidado de no caer sobre las plantas de los pies, y sí sobre las puntas, con el objeto de no ser cójido en descuido y estar pronto para dar dos, tres, cuatro ó mas brincos.

Esta manera de *quitar* es la mas frecuente; pero hay otra que es mas arriesgada, aunque segura, si se acude á tiempo, y consiste en separar con el brazo desarmado el brazo armado del contrario cuando se aprocsima a herir. En los *floretazos* se ejecuta este *quite* con muy buen écsitó, llegando á vezes á cojer por la muñeca el brazo del adversario; por eso advertimos que aquellos golpes deben tirarse muy rápidamente y en disposicion de cortar la mano ó brazo que va á *quitar*, usando al efecto un *cuarto de plumada*.

Tirando con sombrero, se hacen los *quites* con él, intentando desarmar con un fuerte choque la mano que acomete.

Tambien se hace con frecuencia una suerte de quite, que es la mas arriesgada de todas, y

accustomed to the vision to measure the distance, and waiting with tranquility and without fear of the blow that the opponent strikes, when he knows that it has missed by one or half an inch to reach his body.

If the blow comes somewhere into in the *terreno* of the *diestro*, he will be free of it with shrinking the part of the body that is threatened, and without the need to flee or jump. But if the action of the opponent is unknown to the *diestro* because of his speed, or the blow that is struck at him has entered to the center of the *terreno*, he will dodge it with an escape jumping backwards or sidewards, a distance sufficient to not be reached, and if able to, to reach the one who attacks; taking utmost care not to fall on the soles of the feet, but upon the points, with the object to not to be caught in carelessness and be ready to give two, three, four or more jumps.

This manner of *quitar* is the most frequent; but there is another that is more risky, although safe, if you go in time, and consists of putting aside with the unarmed arm the weapon arm of the opponent when he approaches to wound. In the *floretazos* this *quite* is carried out with very good success, arriving at times to take arm of the adversary by the wrist; that's why we warn that those blows must be struck very rapidly and of disposition for cutting the hand or arm that is going to *quitar*, using to the effect a quarter *plumada*.

Fighting with the hat, you make those *quites* with it, trying to disarm with a strong shock the hand that attacks.

Also is done with frequency a type of *quitar*, which is the most risky of all, and

es del modo siguiente. Cuando el brazo armado del contrarío se aproesima al terreno del diestro por la *parte baja*, este se libertará del golpe sacudiéndole una recia patada en los dedos que sostienen la navaja, que se le hará soltar dejandole desarmado. Hemos dicho que es suerte arriesgada, y así es la verdad; pues si fallase al diestro el golpe intentado con el pie, seguramente seria herido por el contrario de una manera terrible, que solo podria remediar, arrojándose al suelo y dándole al mismo tiempo una patada en el bajo vientre.

LECCION UNDECIMA.

RECURSOS.

Cuando al diestro no son suficientes las reglas dadas para libertarse del contrario, ó para acometerle, tiene necesidad de apelar á los *recursos*; llamados asi porque dan salida muchas vezes á lo que la destreza no ha podido hacer.

El arte de manejar la navaja ha establecido algunos que esplicaremos muy por encima, por pertenecer su mayor parte á lo que con el nombre de *tretas* va comprendido en la segunda parte de esta Instruccion.

Bueno es saber que son los *recursos* un suple-reglas que alcanzan á donde estas no; de aquí es que cada diestro pone en ejercicio los que mejor se le adaptan, ó los que é mismo ha inventado.

Daremos á conocer algunos *recursos*.

it is of the following way. When the weapon arm of the opponent approaches the *terreno* of the *diestro* at the lower part, he will be freed from the blow by a strong shocking kick in the fingers that hold the knife, that he will let go leaving him unarmed. We have said that it is risky technique, and that is the truth; for if the *diestro* fails the intended blow with the foot, surely he would be wounded by the opponent in a terrible manner, which has only one remedy, throwing himself to the ground and at the same time giving him a kick in the lower belly.

ELEVENTH LESSON.
RECURSOS [RESPONSES].

When the rules given are not enough for the *diestro* to free himself from the opponent, or to attack him, it is necessary to appeal to the *recursos*; so called because many times they give a way out where skill has not been able to.

The art of handling the *navaja* has established some [*recursos*] above that we will explain further, for the most part belonging with those of the name of *tretas* [tricks] included in the second part of this Instruction.

It is good to know that those *recursos* are supplementary rules that reach where others do not; it is from here that every *diestro* puts into practice those that best adapt to him, or those he has himself invented.

We will give some *recursos* to know.

Pertenecen á lá clase de *recursos*, los *engaños* ó *finjimientos* de que ya hablaremos.

El seconder el diestro sus dos manos detrás del cuerpo, para que el adversario no vea en cuál de ellas se halla la navaja, es un *recurso* de muy buen écsito, mayormente si al sacar la mano armada finje antes sacar la otra. Para hacer bien esta suerte bastará inclinar un poco el cuerpo por el lado del *engaño* y mover en la misma direccion el codo del brazo que engaña: pues el contrario se creerá acometido por aquella parte, y es muy natural que la huya, echando el cuerpo por la otra en la cual deberá recibir el golpe.

El dejarse caer en tierra con la naturalidad propia del que resbala, de modo que el contrario

[Image – engaños]

no sospeche que hay *engaño*, es un *recurso*, que bien ejecutado puede asegurar el fin que el diestro se propone; porque creyendo aquel que este ha caido involuntariamente, puede de buena

Belonging to the class of *recursos*, those *engaños* [deceit] or *finjimientos* that we will talk about.

To hide the *diestro's two hands* behind his body, so that the adversary does not see in which of them he has the *navaja*, is a *recurso* with very good success, especially if before taking out the armed hand [from behind the back] he pretends to take out [feint] the other. To do this technique well it is enough to tilt the body a little to the side of the deceit and move the elbow of the deceiving arm in the same direction: because the opponent will believe he is attacked by that part, and it is very natural to flee, throwing the body to the other [side] in which he must receive the blow.

To fall on the ground with the naturalness of one that slips, in such a way that the opponent

[Image – *engaños*]

does not suspect that it is *engaño*, a *recursos*, well executed this can assure the end that the *diestro* proposes; because believing that he has fallen involuntarily, he [the opponent] can of good

fe arrojarse a el, el cual levantandose con presteza sobre una de las rodillas le recibe con la punta de la navaja hiriendole en el bajo vientre, como representan las anteriores figuras. Es suerte que ecsije mucha lijereza en el diestro; de tal modo, que la hemos visto hacer dejando escapar al mismo tiempo la navaja, para major enganar al adversario, y en el acto de incorporarse recojerla del suelo y a bastanta distancia.

La caida suele hacerse de espalda; y el medio de levantarse es apoyando un pie y la mano desarmada fuertemente en tierra, y con lo restante del cuerpo, dando un violento empuje, situarse en la posicion dicha.

faith throw himself at him [the fallen *diestro*], who rising quickly on one of his knees receives him with the point of the *navaja* wounding him in the lower belly, as the previous figure represents. It is a technique that demands a lot of agility in the *diestro*; in such a way, that we have seen him let the *navaja* escape at the same time, in order to better deceive the adversary, and in the act of sitting up pick it up from the ground and at [just] enough distance.

The fall is usually done backwards; and the means of getting up is supporting one foot and the unarmed hand strongly on the ground, and with the rest of the body, giving a violent push, to stand in the said position.

[Image]

PARTE SEGUNDA.

De las varias suertes que se ejucatan al tirar á la navaja.

LECCION PRIMERA.

GUARDIAS.

La han visto nuestros lectores en la primera parte de esta Instruccion, y con la estension que cabe en un pequeño Manual como el presente, los principales medios de ofensa y defensa que tienen lugar en el ejercicio de la navaja; y decimos los principales medios, porque puede asegurarse que hay tantos como tiradores ó barateros, y fuera trabajo minucioso y dificil el dar una esplicacion completa de cada uno.

Conocidos, pues, los *golpes* y los *quites*, que son lo esencial á nuestro propósito, pasemos ahora á esplicar el modo de ponerlos en ejecucion, una vez colocados frente á frente los combatientes para reñir; es decir que enseñaremos cómo ha de obrar el diestro segun la distinta *guardia* en que se ponga, y qué partido podrá sacar de los conocimientos adquiridos.

Es de tal manera notable lo mucho que la li-

SECOND PART.

Of the several techniques that are executed when striking with the *navaja*.

FIRST LESSON.

GUARDS.

Our readers have seen it in the first part of this Instruction, and to the extent that fits in this small *Manual* as presented, those principle means of offense and defence that have a place in the exercise of the *navaja*; and we say the principle methods, because it is assured that there are as many [methods] as *tiradores* or *barateros*, and it would be meticulous and difficult job to give a complete explanation of each one.

Well-known, then, the blows and the *quites*, that are essential to our purpose, let us now proceed to explain the way to put them into execution, once the combatants have been placed face to face to fight; that is to say that we will teach how the *diestro* must act according to the different guards in which he puts himself, and what benefit he will take from the acquired knowledge.

It is of such a notable manner how much the

jereza de ojos ayuda á toda clase de suertes, que estando en guardia el diestro puede aprocsimarse al contrario hasta tocar en su terreno, y por lo tanto arriesgarse considerablemente á ser herido, siempre que se proponga no permitirle mover el brazo armado; pues al mas insignificante movimiento que hiciese podria herirle en el mismo brazo, obligándole de esta manera á permanecer sin atacar. Esta suerte es de mucho peligro, porque para los dos combatientes solo hay un *terreno* donde ambos pueden herirse sin movimiento alguno de pies, y con estirar el brazo de la navaja.

[Image – terreno]

El diestro se puede colocar en *guardia* usando de cualquiera de las *suertes*, pero con la es-

the agility of the eyes helps all kinds of techniques, that standing on guard the *diestro* can approach the opponent until he touches his *terreno*, and therefore at considerable risk of being wounded, as long as he intends to not allow him to move his weapon arm; for the most insignificant movement he makes he could hurt him in the same arm, forcing him in this manner to remain without attacking. This technique is very dangerous, because for the two combatants there is only one *terreno* where both can be wounded without any movement of feet, and with stretching the arm of the *navaja*.

[Image - *terreno*]

The *diestro* can be placed on guard using any of the techniques, but with the

-presa condicion de no olvidar un instante la posicion en que se encuentra, y de saber los puntos de su cuerpo espuestos al alcanze del brazo armado del contrario.

Hemos visto algunas vezes echarse en tierra al diestro, usando de esta suerte para *guardia*, y es en verdad una de las mas seguras y en la que tiene mas probabilidades de no ser *atracado*, sin riesgo inminente del contrario. El único medio fácil de acometer al que se presenta en esta *guardia* es recibiendo sus golpes con el sombrero en la mano.

[Image – culebra]

Siempre que el diestro acomete á su adversario tiene que hacerlo por la *parte alta* ó por la *parte baja*, como dijimos en su lugar; y de aquí se sigue, que cuando tira un golpe se arriesga á recibir otra en la *parte* contraria á la que acomete; es decir, que si tira á la *parte alta* deja descubierta su *parte baja*, y si tira á la *parte baja* deja al descubierto su *parte alta*.

Se puede admitir como regla jeneral que el

express condition he not forget for an instant the position in which he is in, and of knowing the points of his body exposed to the reach of the weapon arm of the opponent.

We have sometimes seen the *diestro* lying on the ground, using this technique to guard, and it is in truth one of the most secure and it has the most probability of not being attacked, without imminent risk to the opponent. The only easy method of attacking the one who presents in this guard is receiving his blows with the hat in the hand.

[Image – snake]

Whenever the *diestro* attacks his adversary he has to do it to the upper part or to the lower part, as we discussed in its place; and from this it follows that when striking a blow he risks receiving another in the part contrary to the one that he attacks; that is to say, if he strikes the upper part he exposes his lower part, and if he strikes to the lower part he exposes his upper part.

It can be accepted as a general rule that the

momento oportuno en que el diestro debe de herir á su contrario es aquel en que, despues de haber tirado este su golpe, retira el brazo armado que no pudo *hallar carne*, valiéndonos de una espresion que usan los barateros. Es menester mucho aplomo, y aguardar con cautela aquel momento que se aprovechará sin demora; y si no se lográre el objeto, hay que retirarse de pronto y lo mas bajo posible para no ser acometido á su vez en el instante de la retirada.

LECCION SEGUNDA.

GOLPES DE FRENTE.

Vamos ahora á esplicar las puñaladas que tienen lugar en las varias suertes que se ejecutan confundiendo los *terrenos*. Parecerá estraño á muchos de nuestros lectores el que no hayamos hablado de ellas, al tratar de las diversas especies de *golpes* que hemos esplicado en la primera parte de esta Instruccion; pero á esos les diremos, que preferimos esplicar en esta segunda parte los golpes de frente y de *costado* separadamente de todos los demás, porque despúes de hablar en la leccion anterior de las *guardias*, creemos deber hacerlo en esta y la que sigue, de los *golpes* que se tiran con los movimientos que se saben ya.

Por *golpes de frente* entendemos los que se tiran los combatientes cara á cara y sin buscarse los costados ni usar de *tretas*. Puesto en guardia el diestro, se vá aprocsimando á su contrario hasta confundir los *terrenos*, y entonces levancando con presteza el brazo armado le tira una

opportune moment in which the *diestro* must wound his adversary is that in which, after having struck his blow, he withdraws the weapon arm that could not '*find the meat*', using the expression used by the *barateros*. It is necessary to be very composed, and to await with caution that moment that he can take advantage without delay; and if the target is not reached, it [the arm] must be withdrawn quickly and as low as possible so as not to be attacked in turn at the instant of withdrawal.

SECOND LESSON.

BLOWS OF THE FRONT.

Let us now explain the *puñaladas* that take place in the various techniques that are executed when merging the *terrenos*. It will seem strange to many of our readers that we have not spoken of these, in dealing with the different species of blows that we have explained in the first part of this Instruction; but to them we will say, that we prefer to explain in this second part those blows of the front and of the side separately from all the rest, because after speaking in the previous lesson of the guards, we believe we should do in this and the following, of the blows that are struck with the movements that are already known.

By blows of the front we mean those that the combatants strike face to face and without seeking the sides nor using tricks. Once the *diestro* is in guard, he goes approaching his opponent to merge the *terrenos*, and then quickly lifting the weapon arm he strikes a

plumada que llegara a heirirle si no *huye* o *quita*; lo que hara aquel estirando al mismo tiempo el brazo armado para dar un *floretazo*.

[Image – guardias]

LECCION TERCERA.
GOLPES DE COSTADO.

Golpes de costado son los que se tiran los combatientes buscandose los vacios y las costillas, y se dan en los *jiros*, *contrajiros* y muchas vezes en las *corridas*.

LECCION CUARTA.
CORRIDAS.

La *corrida* es una de las suertes mas usuals entre los *tiradores*; y podemos asegurar sin remor de equivocarnos, que es la mas esencial de este

plumada that will reach to wound if he does not flee or *quita*; doing that by stretching out the weapon arm at the same time to give a *floretazo*.

[Image - *guardias*]

THIRD LESSON.
BLOWS OF THE SIDE.

Blows of the side are those that combatants strike seeking those gaps[17] and ribs, and they are given in the *jiros, contrajiros* and many times in the *corridas*.

FOURTH LESSON.
CORRIDAS [RUNS].

The *corrida* is one of the most usual techniques among the *tiradores*; and we can assure without fear of making a mistake, which is the most essential of this

arte, ya porque en si encierra todas las maneras de acometer al contrario, ó como se dice entre los barateros, de *buscarle el bulto*, ya de defenderse ó huir el cuerpo. En ella se tira todá clase de *golpes*, ó mejor dicho, es el arte completo.

La *corrida* no es otra cosa que la descripcion de un semicirculo hecho por cada uno de los combatientes en el acto de la riña; pero procurando siempre conservar la primitiva distancia hasta que llegue el momento de acometer, en cuyo caso habrá necesidad de entrarse en el terreno contrario y herir con cualquiera de los golpes conocidos.

La corrida se ejecuta marchando por uno de los lados indistintamente y sin variar la primera posicion de la guardia, unas vezes por la izquierda otras por la derecha; pues siempre que uno de los *tiradores* ataca al otro, el acometido *jira* ó *huye* con la *corrida* por el lado opuesto, ó se sale del *terreno* brincando. De aquí resulta que los dos semicírculos que forman los combatientes, uno enfrente del otro, llegan á describir un circulo entero, mas ó menos perfecto, y de una variada visualidad.

Cuanta mayor lijereza tenga el diestro en sus pies, tanto mejor se ejecutará la *corrida*, porque como ya dijimos, este arte estriba mas en la ajilidad y sangre fria del diestro que en ninguna otra cosa; pues aunque el uso es muy esencial, de nada serviria sin el ausilio de esas dos cualidades.

LECCION QUINTA.

MOLINETE.

Cuando el contrario se arroja demasiado sobre el diestro, deberá este usar del *molinete*, que

art, because it contains all the manners of attacking the opponent, or as it is said among the *barateros*, to '*seek the bulge*'[18], either for defending or [a]voiding with the body. In it are struck all kinds of blows, or better said, it is the complete art.

The *corrida* is nothing other than the describing of a semicircle made by each of the combatants in the act of the fight; but trying always to maintain the original distance until reaching the moment for the attack, in which case there will be a need to enter the opponent's *terreno* and wound with any of the known blows.

The *corrida* is executed by marching on one of the sides indistinctly and without changing the original position of the guard, some times on the left others on the right; for whenever one of the *tiradores* attacks the other, the attacked turns or voids with the *corrida* on the opposite side, or jumps out of the *terreno*. From here it follows that the two semicircles formed by the combatants, one in front of the other, come to describe an entire circle, more or less perfect, and of a varied aesthetic.

The more agility the *diestro* has on his feet, the better the *corrida* will be executed, because as we have already said, this art lies more in the agility and cold blood of the *diestro* than in any other thing; although the action is most essential, it is of no service without the assistance of these two qualities.

FIFTH LESSON.
MOLINETE [WHEEL].

When the opponent throws himself too much upon the *diestro*, he must use the *molinete*, which

consiste en levantar del suelo uno de los pies, sobre el otro jirar todo el cuerpo en derredor con mucha velozidad, y parándole de pronto, estirar el brazo armado para dar un *floretazo* al que le acomete.

Téngase presente que es suerte muy peligrosa, y que la ocasion mas oportuna para ejecutarla es cuando el adversario tira el *golpe* por bajo, no debiendo hacerse cuando el golpe viene por alto; pues ya hemos dicho que el floretazo se tira casi siempre á la *parte alta*, y para ello se necesita que el golpe del contrario amague á la *parte baja*.

Si el diestro se halla muy *cerrado* por su parte alta, es decir, si es acometido por el contrario muy dentro del *terreno propio*, le recibirá bajando el cuerpo hasta colocarse con una rodilla en tierra y presentándole la navaja ácia el bajo vientre. Véase la figura de la leccion undécima, parte primera.

Tenemos que advertir que tanto en el *molinete* como en los *floretazos* altos se espone el diestro á que le coja su brazo armado, el brazo desarmado del adversario, quien volviéndole con fuerza su muñeca acia la garganta podrá herirle cón su misma navaja.

consists in lifting one of the feet off the ground, upon the other turning the whole body around great speed, and stopping suddenly, stretching the weapon arm to give a *floretazo* to the attacker.

Bear in mind that it is a very dangerous technique, and that the most opportune occasion to execute it is when the adversary strikes the low blow, it must not be done when the blow comes high; for we have already said that the *floretazo* is almost always struck to the upper part, and for this it is necessary that the blow of the opponent threatens the lower part.

If the *diestro* finds he is very closed on his high part, that is, if he is attacked by an opponent very much within his own *terreno*, he will receive it lowering his body until he places himself with one knee on the ground and presenting the *navaja* to the lower belly. See the figure of the eleventh lesson, part one.

We have to warn that both in the *molinete* and in the high *floretazos* the *diestro* exposes his weapon arm to be caught, [by] the unarmed arm of the adversary, who by turning his wrist with force towards his throat can wound him with his own *navaja*.

[Image]

LECCION SESTA.

LANZAR LA NAVAJA.

Entre muchos *tiradores*, y mas comunmente entre los marineros, se acostumbra lanzar la navaja al cuerpo del contrario, la cual llevan sujeta á la cintura con un largo cordou ó cadenilla de alambre.

Parecerá increible á algunos de nuestros lectores la prodijiosa puntería con que hemos visto lanzar la navaja, dejándola clavada en el pecho ó vientre, y precisamente en el punto que la vista del diestro habia señalado; pero nada hay mas cierto, y tan admirable habilidad solo es comparable con la que manifiesta aquel á quien la navaja se dirije, llegando en muchos casos á libertarse del *golpe*, y hasta cojer el cordon que la sujeta y cortarle con la suya.

Nosotros á la par que admiramos tanta ajilidad destreza, aconsejamos á los tiradores que nunca usen de esta suerte por lo incierta y peligrosa que es; á pesar de haber hombres que la ejecutan con tal acierto, y que solo debe atribuirse al continuado ejercido que en ello tienen desde muchachos.

LECCION SETIMA.

PASES DE MANO Y DE SOMBRERO.

Puesto que ya hemos visto que la fijeza y prontitud de la vista es lo que mas contribuyen al buen manejo de la navaja, esplicaremos el me-

SIXTH LESSON.

THROWING THE NAVAJA.

Among many *tiradores*, and more commonly among sailors, it is customary to throw the *navaja* at the body of the opponent, which is fastened at the waist with a long cord or wire chain.

It will seem incredible to some of our readers the prodigious aim with which we have seen the *navaja* thrown, leaving it nailed in the chest or belly, and precisely in the point that the vision of the *diestro* had specified; but there is nothing more true, and such admirable ability is only comparable to that displayed by the one at whom the knife is thrown, who in many cases can free himself from the blow, and even grabbing the cord that secures it and cutting it off with his own.

While we at the same time admire such agile skill, we advise the *tiradores* to never use this technique because of how uncertain and dangerous it is; despite having men who perform it with such success, and that should only be attributed to the continued practice that they have had since they were boys.

SEVENTH LESSON.

PASSES OF THE HAND AND OF THE HAT.

Since we have already seen that the steadiness and quickness of the sight is what contributes the most to the good handling of the *navaja*, we will explain the

-dio de que se valen los tiradores para obligar al contrario á variarla ó a cerrar los ojos. Después que el diestro ha finjido ó tirado algunos golpes, y quiere desviar la vista del adversario para acometerle; en el mismo momento que lo hiciere, ó bien se pasará la mano desarmada por delante de los ojos ó por los de aquel, ó bien tomando el sombrero que llevará en la cabeza lo pasará una ó mas vezes de la misma manera, en cuyo instante se arrojará sobre él por la parte baja á herirle en el vientre.

LECCION OCTAVA.

RECORTES.

El *recorte* no es mas que un *jiro*, con la diferencia de que el diestro al ejecutarlo da la espalda al contrario, mientras que el *jiro* require que se haga dando siempre el frente.

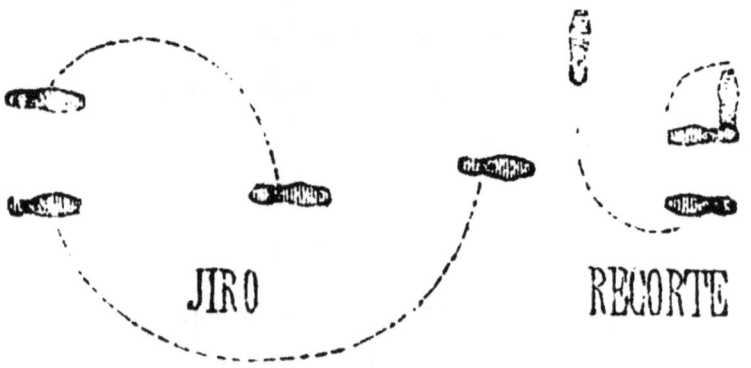

Tiene lugar cuando el diestro es acometido con un *jiro* ácia espinazo, y es muy espuesto.

means that are valued by the *tiradores* used to force the opponent to flinch or close their eyes. After the *diestro* has feinted or struck some blows, and wants to divert the view of the adversary for an attack; at the same moment that he does, either he will pass the unarmed hand in front of or towards the eyes, or taking the hat from his head to pass it one or more times in the same manner, at which instant he will launch upon him to the lower part to wound him in the belly.

EIGHTH LESSON.
RECORTES [CUTAWAYS].

The *recorte* is no more than a *jiro*, with the difference that the *diestro* when executing it turns his back on the opponent, while the *jiro* requires that it be done by always giving the front.

[Image]

It takes place when the *diestro* is attacked with a *jiro* towards the spine, and is very exposed.

LECCION NOVENA.

SUERTE DE LA CULEBRA.

La suerte de la *culebra* consiste en arrojarse de pechos al suelo el diestro que la va á ejecutar, y apoyado en la mano desarmada ir andando ácia el terreno del contrario á herirle en su bajo vientre con *floretazo* ó *plumada*.

LECCION DECIMA.

ENGANOS.

Todo *golpe* puede ser verdadero ó finjido.

Se llama verdadero, cuando la intencion del que le tira, es herir á su adversario.

Es finjido, cuando el diestro lo marca solamente con el fin de engañar y cojer desprevenido á su contrario.

Así, pues, en las *puñaladas de frente*, se finjirá el golpe á la parte baja, para poder herir con acierto en la *parte alta*, y vice versa; pues amagado el diestro por alto acudirá naturalmente al mismo punto con su navaja, si no conoce el engaño, y quedará descubierto por lo bajo á donde irá el golpe verdadero; y amagado por lo bajo acudirá allí con su mano armada, yendo entonces el golpe á lo alto y jeneralmente á *enfilar*.

Se puede establecer por regla jeneral, que todo golpe verdadero puede convertirse en *golpe*

NINTH LESSON

TECHNIQUE OF THE SNAKE.

The technique of the snake consists of the *diestro* who is going to execute it throwing his chest to the ground, and leaning on the unarmed hand to moving towards the *terreno* of the opponent to wound him in his lower belly with *floretazo* or *plumada*.

TENTH LESSON.

DECEITS.

Every blow can be true or feigned.

It is called true, when the intention of the one who strikes, is to wound his adversary.

It is feigned, when the *diestro* marks it only with the purpose of deceiving and surprising [catching unprepared] his opponent.

So, then, in the stabs to the front, he feints the blow to the lower part, to be able to wound successfully in the upper part, and vice versa; then, the *diestro* threatening high he [opponent] will naturally come to the same point with his *navaja,* if he does not know the deception, and he will leave the low uncovered to where the true blow will go; and threatening low he will go there with his weapon hand, and the blow then goes high and generally to *enfilar.*

It can be established as general rule, that all true blows can become

fínjido ó sea *engaño*, y todo golpe finjido convertirse en golpe verdadero.

Se pueden igualmente finjir los jiros y contrajiros, y asi el diestro, por ejemplo, hará uno finjido por cualquier lado, con el cual, engañado su contrario hará el contrajiro correspondiente, presentando de este modo descubierto el lado á donde irá el golpe verdadero.

LECCION UNDECIMA.
TRETAS.

Hemos llegado alpunto en que con razon nos pondremos de parte de los que aborrezen el manejo de la navaja. Seguramente que si no atendiésemos á otra cosa que á lo que resulta del uso de algunas *tretas* que ponen en práctica ciertos tiradores, debiéramos acusar de inmoral y altamente innoble su ejercicio; pero ya han visto nuestros lectores las reglas fundamentales que hemos dado en el curso de nuestras lecciones, y conocerán que no todo en el arte de tirar á la navaja es vil y reprobado, y que por el contrario, se le debe considerar sujeto á principios jenerales como el de cualquiera otra arma. No quisiéramos nosotros que, por la relacion de varias *tretas* de que se valen muchos hombres degradados y cobardes, se formase una ídea equivocada de los *tiradores* de navaja, cuando el abuso que de ella hacen aquellos no pertenece al arte; los que asi obran con la navaja obrarían del mismo modo con un florete ó con un sable. Por lo tanto nos abstenemos de indicarlas por lo repugnantes que aparecen á nuestros ojos, y por lo

feints or deceiving blows, and all blows feinted become true blows.

One can equally feign the *jiros* and *contrajiros*, and so the *diestro*, for example, will make a feint on either side, with which, his opponent deceived will make the corresponding *contrajiro*, in this way presenting uncovered the side to where the true blow will go.

ELEVENTH LESSON.
TRICKS.

We have come to the point where we will with reason take the side of those who abhor the handling of the *navaja*. Surely that if we did not attend to anything other than what results from the use of some tricks put into practice by certain *tiradores*, we should condemn their practice as immoral and highly ignoble; but our readers have already seen the fundamental rules that we have given in the course of our lessons, and they will know that not all in the art of striking with the *navaja* is vile and reprobate, and that on the contrary, it must be considered subject to general principles like any other weapon. We do not desire that, by the connection of various tricks that are valued greatly by degraded and cowardly men, a wrong idea be formed of the *tiradores* of the *navajas*, when the abuse done by them does not belong to the art; those who thus work with the *navaja* would work in the same way with a foil or a sabre. Therefore we refrain from indicating them because they appear repugnant to our eyes, and so

dístante que están del objeto que nos propusimos al escribir esta *Manual*; mas no nos es posible al mismo tiempo, prescindir de hablar de algunas que creemos adaptables en casos de apuro, ó que conviene que las evite el hombre acometido injustamente.

Ya hemos dicho en la primera parte, que con la faja que el diestro debe llevar á la cintura se ejecutan algunas tretas, y asi es la verdad. En las varias *corridas* que se hacen en riña, cuando el diestro quiere practicar una treta con su faja, no tiene mas que soltar el estremo de ella y dejarla arrastrar por el suelo, de manera que su contrario fácilmente la pise, en cuyo caso tirando velozmente de ella le hará caer en tierra ó tropezar malamente.

Otra treta se ejecuta con la faja, y es: llevando en el estremo de ella dinero, piedras, ó cualquier cosa que la haga bastante pesada, la arrojará el diestro con violencia á las piernas de su adversario, el cual se encontrará trabado y sin poder moverse, quedando en disposicion de ser herido.

El sombrero se arroja á la cara del contrario, y es treta de muy buen efecto.

Algunas vezes el diestro recoje un puñado de tierra, si en el lugar de la riña la hubiere, y le tira á los ojos del adversario, yéndole á *atracar* sin demora.

El diestro puede también pisar con uno de sus pies otro del contrario, y es treta de buen écsito si no se evita.

Puede también el diestro dar á su contrario una fuerte patada en el vientre, ó enredar con sus piernas las de aquel, haciéndole dar en tierra.

distant they are from the objective that we proposed to write this *Manual*; but it is not possible for us at the same time, to to do without talking about some that we believe are adaptable in case of trouble, or that are advisable to avoid men who would attack unjustly.

We have already said in the first part, that with the sash that the *diestro* must wear at the waist he can execute some tricks, and that is the truth. In the various *corridas* that are made in the fight, when the *diestro* wants to practice a trick with his sash, he has but to loosen the end of it and leave it to drag on the ground, in a manner that his opponent can easily step on it, in which case pulling it quickly will make him fall to the ground or stumble badly.

Another trick can be executed with the sash, and it is: carrying in the end of it money, stones, or anything that makes it heavy enough, the *diestro* will throw it violently at the legs of his adversary, who will find himself stuck and unable to move, remaining in position to be wounded.

The hat is thrown into the face of the opponent, and is a trick of very good effect.

Sometimes the *diestro* picks up a handful of earth, if there is [any] at the place of the fight, and throws it at the eyes of the adversary, going to the attack without delay.

The *diestro* is also able to tread with one foot upon another of the opponent's, and it is a trick of good success if it is not avoided.

Also the *diestro* can give his opponent a strong kick in the belly, or tangle up his legs with own, making him hit the ground.

El diestro puede desviar su vista de la del contrario, y dirijirla ácia la parte de atrás de éste, el cual creyendo que mira á alguno que está á su espalda, vuelve la cabeza y en el punto es *atracado*.

"*Tente, que vas á tropezar*" dice el diestro á su contrario, con el objeto de que se dirija á mirar al suelo, y en el acto le hiere.

Por último, son tantas las tretas que emplean los tiradores, que se necesitaria mucho tiempo para esplicarlas todas; y así nos contentamos con haber puesto las mas communes y jenerales.

The *diestro* can divert his sight from that of the opponent, and direct it towards the back of him, who, believing that he is looking at someone that is behind him, turns his head and at that point is attacked.

"Stop, you are going to stumble," says the *diestro* to his opponent, with the objective that he directs his gaze at the ground, and in the act wound him.

Finally, there are so many tricks that are employed by *tiradores*, that it would need a long time to explain them all; and so we content ourselves with having put here the most common and general.

[Image]

PARTE TERCERA.

LECCION PRIMERA.
DEL CUCHILLO.

Poco tenemos que decir del *cuchillo* o *puñal*, estando se manejo sujeto en la mayor parte a las reglas que hemos dado para tirar a la navaja. Solamente tendremos que advertir, que los golpes del cuchillo son siempre de punta, y que no reciben otro nombre que el de *puñaladas*.

El cuchillo lo usan mucho los marineros; y en las carceles y presidios es arma con la que cobran el barato frecuentemente los matones.

LECCION SEGUNDA.
POSICIONES.

La planta mas segura para manejar el cuchillo o puñal es la que representan las figuras de la pajina siguiente. El cuchillo se toma con la mano derecha y de la manera que mejor acomode al diestro; en el brazo izquierdo se lia la capa, chaqueta o manta, o bien se coloca, como lo hacen los barateros, una red de cañas o un cuero de bastante resistencia, con lo que se paran las puna-

THIRD PART.

FIRST LESSON.
OF THE KNIFE.

We have little to say of the knife or *puñal*, the subject being handled in most part in the rules that we have given for striking with the *navaja*. We will only warn that, that the blows of the knife are always of the point, and that they do not receive any other name than that of stabs.

The knife is most used by sailors; and in prisons and fortresses it is a weapon with which the thugs frequently barter.

SECOND LESSON.
POSITIONS.

The safest stance for handling the knife or stiletto is the one represented by the figures of the following page. The knife is taken with the right hand and in the manner most accommodating to the *diestro*; on the left arm is rolled the coat, jacket or blanket, or like the *barateros* do, is placed a net of cane or leather of enough resistance[19], with which he stops the stabs

—ladas y se cubre la vista del contrario. La planta no es la misma que se usa en el tiro de navaja, pues en el manejo de cuchillo se coloca el diestro con el brazo y la pierna izquierda sacados al frente del contrario.

A falta de otra cosa con que cubrir el brazo desarmado se usa poner el sombrero o gorra en la mano. Por lo demas es igual en un todo a lo que se ha dicho para la navaja.

LECCION TERCERA.
GOLPES, MODO DE LANZAR EL PUNAL.

Los golpes con el cuchillo o puñal se dan siempre con una mano, es decir, que no hay *cambios*, y por lo mismo van dirijidos acia el lado desarmado del contrario, cuidando de herir en la costado izquierdo, que es lo mas seguro.

Los *jiros* tambien se ejecutan con muy buen

and covers the view of the opponent. The stance is not the same as that used in the striking of the *navaja*, because in the handling of the knife the *diestro* is placed with the left arm and leg out in front of the opponent.

In the absence of other things to cover the unarmed arm it is used to put the hat or cap in the hand. For the rest it is equal in all that has been said for the *navaja*.

THIRD LESSON.

BLOWS, WAY OF THROWING THE THRUST.

The blows with the knife or stiletto are always given with one hand, that is to say, that there are no *cambios*, and for the same reason are directed towards the unarmed side of the opponent, taking care of wounding on the left side, which is the safest.

The *jiros* also are executed with very good

ecsito, aunque solamente tienen lugar los del lado derecho, como igualmente el *contrjiro* izquierdo.

El cuchillo se lanza al cuerpo del contrario estendiendole sobre la palma de la mano y con el mango acia fuera; y asi puesto, se arroja con impetus y se lo clava, a no ser que huya el cuerpo brincando o echandose en tierra.

LECCION CUARTA.
QUITES, HUIDAS.

Los *quites* y las *huidas* son esactamente iguales a los del manejo de la navaja; --observese lo que va esplicado en aquel lugar.

LECCION QUINTA.
RECURSOS Y TRETAS.

Vease lo que dijimos al hablar de los *recursos* y *tretas* de la navaja.

LECCION SESTA.
DEFENSAS DEL PUNAL.

Si en alguna occasion se encontrase el diestro sin cuchillo, como suele suceder, y se le presentase uno de los muchos hombres que hay de mala intencion con un puñal o cuchillo en la mano; lo que debe hacer es esperarle en guardia de sombrero por el lado derecho, pero sin el y con el brazo levantado, de manera que la mano

success, although only place those on the right side, as equally the left *contrjiros*.

The knife is thrown at the body of the opponent extended over the palm of the hand and with the handle to the outside; and so placed, he throws himself with impetus and drives[20] it in, unless the body voids by jumping or dropping onto the ground.

FOURTH LESSON.
RETREATS, ESCAPES.

The retreats and the escapes are exactly the same as those from the handling of the *navaja*; -- Observe what is explained in that place.

FIFTH LESSON.
RESPONSES AND TRICKS.

See what we said in talking of the *recursos* and *tretas* of the *navaja*.

SIXTH LESSON.
DEFENCES OF THE STAB.

If on any occasion the *diestro* finds himself without a knife, as often happens, and one of the many men who are of bad intention present themselves to him with a stiletto or a knife in his hand; what he should do is wait for him in the guard of the hat[21] on the right side, but without it [the hat] and with the arm raised, of the manner that the hand

este aun mas altra que las cabeza, descubriendo todo el pecho, como lo manifestan las siguientes figuras; y cuando el contrario le tire la puñalada, se defendera el diestro dandole con la mano un golpe en la muneca, y si puede ser agarrandosela por debajo; y si no, no desunirse; y al mismo tiempo huir el pie izquierdo formando con el cuerpo concavidad, y levantando el derecho

[Image – sin cuchillo]

para sentarle detras del izquierdo de su contrario; haciendo centro en el izquierdo, le echara la mano izquierda al cogote, procurando hacer todos los movimientos sin temor, y muy prontos, y se lograra la defensa. Y si hallandose el contrario en esta disposicion por haberle salido fallida su resolucion, se fuese a retirar para volver a acometer, el diestro en aquel mismo tiempo le ayudara a levanter, empujandole para que su mismo instrumento le sea en su perjucio.

is even higher than the head, uncovering the whole chest, as the shown by the following figures; and when the opponent strikes the thrust, the *diestro* will defend with the hand giving a blow on the wrist, and grab underneath if it can be; and if not, do not separate; and at the same time void the left foot forming concave with the body, and lifting the right

[Image – without a knife]

to sit behind the left of the opponent; making a center[22] on the left, he will throw the left hand to the neck, trying to make all movements without fear, and very quickly, and the defence will be achieved. And if the opponent is found in this position for having failed his resolution[23], he will retreat to attack again, the *diestro* at that same time will help him to rise, pushing him so that his own instrument becomes his perjury.

PARTE CUARTA.

LECCION PRIMERA.
DE LAS TIJERAS.

Los jitanos son los unicos que manejan esta clase de arma, sin duda porque jeneralmente dedicados al trafico y comercio de caballeras la llevan consigo para esquilar las mulas y pollinos. Hay tambien esquiladores aragoneses.

Escusamos decribir aqui se mecanismo, pues ninguno de nuestros lectores dejará de conocerle.

LECCION SEGUNDA.
MODO DE MANEJARLAS.

El modo de manejar las tijeras en riña, es iqual al del cuchillo que ya hemos esplicado; y solo tenemos que añadir que, cojidas por el centro que forman sus cuatro patas cuando estan abiertas, la herida que causan es comunmente con las dos puntas, y siempre mortal.

Nada mas tenemos que decir del manejo de esta arma que no vaya dicho en el de la navaja y en el del cuchillo, teniendo en ella lugar su aplicacion, y siendo las reglas communes á las tres armas.

FOURTH PART.

FIRST LESSON.
OF THE SCISSORS.

The *jitanos* are the only ones who handle this kind of weapon, without doubt because they are dedicated generally to the trade and commerce of the horses, they carry with them to shear the mules and donkeys[24]. There are also Aragonese shearers.

Excuse here our need to describe the mechanism, as none of our readers will know it.

SECOND LESSON.
THE WAY OF HANDLING.

The way to handle the scissors in the fight, is equal to that of the knife that we have already explained; and we have only to add that, taken by the center that forms the four legs when they are open, the wound that they cause is commonly with both points, and always deadly.

Nothing more have we to say of the handling of this weapon that is not said in the *navaja* and the knife, having in its place its application, and the rules being common to the three weapons.

EL BARATERO

Tipos sumamente particulares tiene España que pueda decirse no se encuentran semejantes ni aun parecidos en otras naciones; pero ninguno tan marcado como el baratero, ó sea el maton que saca un impuesto forzoso en los circulos de los tahúres que se llaman garitos. Este personaje truanesco nacido regularmente de la hez del pueblo, y criado en las carceles y presidios, tiene con frecuencia un fin trájico, acarreado por sus azanas ya sea en medio de una playa ó de un hejido a manos de otro mas valiente ó mas afortunado que él, que el *arrebaña* el mondongo ante un público formado de charranes, soldados, ladrones y *gachés*; ya en el centro de una plazuela ó escampado, encima de un tablado de alguna elevacion y á manos del ejecutor de la justicia, el cual despues del *¿me perdonas?* consabido, le aprieta y descompone la *canería del pan* con el mayor desenfado del mundo, aplicandole al suello un *corbatin de Vizcaya*.

Tres son pues, las clases de barateros conocidos: el baratero de tropa, el de la carcel, y el de la playa; y vamos á hablar de ellos separadamente. El *baratero de tropa*, educado en los cuarteles y cantinas donde hizo su trabajoso aprendizaje, es conocido en el acto por su aire ternejal y de perdona-vidas, su apostura maja, siempre con un *pitoche* ó cigarro en la boca y otro sostenido

THE BARATERO

It can be said that Spain has very particular types [of people] and similar are not found nor even apparent in other nations; but none so remarkable as the *baratero*, that is the thug that imposes a forced tax in the circles of the craven that are called gambling dens. These dishonest persons regularly born of the scum of society, and raised in prisons and fortresses, often having a tragic end, brought about as a result of their previous exploits in the means of smuggling or wounded at the hands of another braver or more fortunate than he, that of disembowelment in front of a gathering of rascals, soldiers, thieves and cowboys; already in the center of a plaza or empty ground, upon an elevated platform and at the hands of the executor of justice, who after the usual "*forgive me?*"[25], he squeezes [twists the executioner's handle] and breaks the wind pipe[26] with the greatest ease in the world, applying to the neck a Vizcaya bowtie[27].

Three are thus, the classes of known *barateros*: the *baratero* of the troop, that of the jail, and that of the beach [smugglers]; and we will talk about them separately. The *baratero* of the troop, educated in the barracks and *cantinas* where he made his laborious apprenticeship, he is known on the spot by his bullying and high and mighty attitude, his attractive good looks, always with a whistle [cigarette] or cigar in the mouth and another held

en la oreja, pelo mas largo que todos los soldatos de su compañía, la gorra de cuartel ladeada, la casaca sin abotonar por el pecho, y el cuello de ella doblado ácia a fuera, una mano en el bolsillo del pantalon y la otra colocada sobre la cadera y enseñando en el dedo meñique un anillo de laton; escupe por el colmillo y habla andaluz y *caló*, es muy moreno, casi siempre feo, y si es bizco, mejor; lleva el bigote unas vezes corto, y otras retorcido á lo borgoñon; habla guiñando el ojo y meneando una pierna. Es el *temeron* de la compañía, y el sarjento primero le releva de la mecanica del cuartel, porque en ocasiones necesita dinero, y el baratero le franquea su bolsilli, que está repleto, merced á las trampas y puñaladas en que es tan enttendido, y le han alcanzado alto renombre y gran poer entre sus *camarás*. El baratero de la compania es el mas holgazan de ella, sabe mal el ejercicio y desprecia completamente la ordenanza; pero en cambio maneja como ninguno la *herramienta*, juega á las *chapas* y á la brisca, al cané, á la treinta y una, bebe y trienfa, tiene moza, que es la cantinera del cuartel, y se hace obedecer de todos. En tiempo de compana se bate como el primero, porque es valiente, y no queda el ultimo para el *pillaje*, porque es largo de unas.

En los pueblos donde pára, busca los garitos, y en ellos hace sus ensayos entre la jente mas perdida con quien se relaciona amistosamente, la cual suele pagar su cariño y simpatías con una paliza ó un par de puñaladas, que alcanza por alguna *fullería* no muy limpia.

Este baratero es enemigo nato de los paisanos, á quienes llama patrones; por un quitame allá esas pajas mete mano al primero que topa y

behind his ear, hair longer than all the soldiers of his company, the barracks cap lopsided, the jacket unbuttoned at the chest, and the collar of it folded outwards, one hand in the pocket of his pants and the other placed on his hip and showing a brass ring on his little finger; he spits through his teeth and speaks Andalusian and Calo[28], he is very dark, almost always ugly, and moreso if he is cross-eyed; he has a moustache that is at times short, and others it is twisted into the Burgundian[29]; He talks with a wink of the eye and shake of a leg. He is the bully of the company, and the first sergeant relieves him from the duties of the barracks, because on occasion he needs money, and the *baratero* crosses his palm, which is filled, thanks to the tricks and stabs in which he is so expert, and he has achieved high reknown and great influence among his comrades. The *baratero* of the company is the laziest of them, knows the drills poorly and completely disregards orders; but instead he handles the *herramienta* like no other, he plays the coins and the card games, at thirty-one, drinking and trumps, he has a girl, who is the *cantinera* of the barracks, and he makes all obey him. In times of campaign he fights like the best, because he is brave, and never leaves the pillaging till last, because he has long fingers[30].

In the towns where he stops, he looks for the gambling dens, and in them he makes his swindles among the players who have lost the most, with whom he relates amicably, which for these affections and sympathies he usually pays with a beating or a couple of stabs, which is a result of some dirty cheating.

This *baratero* is the natural enemy of his countrymen, whom he calls patrons; for in the twinkling of an eye[31] he grabs the first one that he encounters and

que él cree le ha *diquelado* con malos *clisos*, y arma un zipizape de todos los diablos. El coronel se entera del escándalo y le mete en un calabozo, del que sale á los dos dias mas *terne y echao pa alantre* y en disposicion de *armarla* con *cualsiquiera*. Pega una paliza diaria á su querida, y la abandona por la del cabo furriel, que se viene con él, y á quien corta la *fila* á la primera infidelidad que le hace.

Cuando el rejimiento pernocta en alguna poblacion, es visitado el baratero de cada compañía por los barateros que hay allí, que muchas vezes son desertores de presidio que se hallan ocultos sin *olfatearlo* la justicia; se llaman *camaráas ó compares*, y van á beber juntos unas copas ó *cañitas* que se tiran á la cara á la mas pequeña contradiccion ó jesto desabrido; se salen á la calle, y empuñando los *alfileres*, se tiran dos ó tres *mojadas* que sirven para que la amistad eche entre ellos hondas raizes; se presentan mútuamente en los garitos en que *mandan ó comen*, pero con la espresa condicion de no *inquietar á naide*, ni querer cobrar los *chavos* donde los cobra su *camará*.

Sigamos con el *baratero de la carcel*. Este es del jénero mas temido de todos. De muchacho ha sido matachin, en cuyo oficio aprendió tódós los modos de *destripar*, las horas que tenia libres, que eran las mas, se entretenía en saquear los bolsillos, del prójimo elegante, ó de cualquiera que le deparaba la suerte indistintamente; conocía á la primera ojeada al patan ó paleto; enganábale bajo cualquier pretesto y le *espantaba* los *parnées*, sin que lo advirtiera, los cuales iba á jugar al cané con otros muchachos á quienes ganaba lo que tenian, á fuerza de trampas y de ame-

that he believes has caught onto him with a dirty look, and with the knife he makes a squabble like the Devil. The colonel finds out about the scandal and puts him in a cell, from which he leaves after two days, even more stubborn and menacing, and of the disposition to fight with anybody. He gives a daily beating to his mistress, and abandons her for the woman of the Corporal Quartermaster, who goes with him, and who he cuts loose at the first infidelity that she makes.

When the regiment stays overnight in any village, the *baratero* of the company is visited by each of the *barateros* there, who many times are deserters of the military who hide themselves to avoid being sniffed out by justice; they are called comrades or compadres, and they go together to drink cups[32] that are thrown in each others' face at the smallest contradiction or disrespectful joke; they go out into the street, and grasping their *alfileres*, they throw two or three stabbing wounds that serve to build a profound connection of the friendship between them; they present themselves mutually in the gambling dens in which they eat or are in charge of, but with the express condition of not disturbing anyone, nor swindling money where the other sleeps.

Let us continue with the *baratero* of the jail. This is the most feared kind of all. As a boy he was a bully, in which trade he learned all the ways to disembowel; the hours he had free, which were most, he entertained himself in looting the pockets, of elegant neighbours, or of anyone that fate brought to him; knowing at first quick glance the uncouth or coarse [easy marks]; deceiving them under any pretext and would without warning frighten the money from them, then with that money go to play cards with other boys from whom he would take what they had, by force of tricks and

-nazas obscenas. Si á pesar de todo era él el perdidoso, allí de su jenio y sus manos, tiraba del pincho y lograba que á la fuerza le entregaran sus caudales, lo cual le iba dando nombradía entre los pilletes y *gatería* de la ciudad. Así fué aumentando en años y picardías, dejando el pabellon bien puesto en las tabernas, cárceles y garitos, donde su fama era colosal. Por último, sentada ya su reputacion, y haciéndose temer de todos los ternejales del matadero, lo llevaron por vijésima vez al *estarivél* sus fechorías y mala lengua. Puesto en él, no se contentó con una posicion brillante entre los presos, sinó que aspiró á mas y lo alcanzó: estaban jugando en el patio á las chapas como una veintena de ellos, y mi hombre llega al corro, tose de una manera particular, y con voz ronca y sosegada pregunta, mirando de reojo a una enorme navaja que estaba hincada en el suelo:

- "¿De quién es esa friolera?

- Mía, repuso el dueño de ella con un jesto que daba horror, y *naide come aquí sinó yo.*

- *Pues, camara, me jace mal al estómago y la quiéo gomitar,* y dándola con el pie la hizo rodar un buen trecho por el suelo.

Allí fué Troya, ánimas benditas! el que cobraba los *chavos* defendió valientemente su derecho adquirido, pero no tanto que mi *Chato* (algun nombre le habremos de dar), entrándole la *herramienta* por el vientre, no le echára el cuajar al aire con grande admiracion de tan honrados circunstantes. Desde entonces es el *baratero* de la cárcel y nadie le tose, cumpliendo con su deber sin que mala *mui* le quite la honra.

¿Quereis, lectores curiosos, conocer al buen *Chato* entre aquella multitud que se rebulle en el

obscene threats. If he was the one to lose in spite of everything, from his wits and his hands, he pulled the *pincho* and force them to hand over their fortunes, which earned him renown among the rascals and gamblers of the city. Thus as he grew in years and cunning, leaving his mark in the taverns, jails and gambling dens, where his fame was colossal. Finally, having built his reputation, and making himself feared by all the rogues of the slaughterhouse, he was taken for the twentieth time to jail for his misdeeds and bad language. Once in it, he was not satisfied with a brilliant position among the prisoners, but he aspired to more and reached it: a score of them were playing in the yard at the game of coins, and our man arrives at the circle, coughs in his particular manner, and with a threatening and calm voice he asks, looking sideways at an enormous *navaja* that was stuck in the ground:

- "Whose is that little thing?

- Mine, replied the owner of the *navaja* with an horrific expression, and no one eats here but me.

- Well, comrade, it makes me sick to the stomach and I want to vomit; and kicking the *navaja* making it roll a good way on the ground.

There was Troy[33], blessed souls! The one who charged the money bravely defended his acquired right, but not so well that our Chato (we must give him some name), his *herramienta* penetrating the belly, the blow curdles the air with great admiration of such honoured bystanders. Since then he has been the *baratero* of the jail and no one has coughed at him, doing what he must without ill luck to remove his honour.

Do you want, curious readers, to meet good Chato among that crowd that is stirring in the

patio? Mirad, allí á la derecha, entre aquel corro de pelgares… ya disteis con él. Su estatura es mas bien pequeña que alta, ancho de espaldas, la fisonomía repugnante y estúpida, muy more-

-no, grandes patillas y largos tufos sobre la frente que lleva recojidos ácia un lado, y algo caídos sobre la ceja izquierda. Su traje está en completa, proporcion con su figura; ancho pantalon de pana verde sostenido en la cintura por una disforme faja de estambre, que es á la vez su pequeño maletin en donde guarda los dineros, la *tea* y la baraja; calza alpargatas ó borceguíes de becerro bastante grotescos; está comunmente en mangas de camisa, y lleva atado al rededor de

yard? Behold, there on the right, among that circle of ruffians… you already met with him. His stature is rather more short than tall, wide of shoulders, his appearance disgusting and stupid, very dark,

[Image]

large sideburns and long tufts on the forehead that is gathered to one side, and somewhat fallen over the left eyebrow. His garb is complete, in full proportion with his figure; wide pants of green corduroy held at the waist by a disheveled sash of wool, which is at the same time his small bag[34] where he guards his money, *tea* [knife] and a deck [of cards]; wedge sandals or grotesque calfskin boots; he is commonly in shirt sleeves[35], and tied around

la cabeza un pañuelo de yerbas que le dá un aspecto siniestro y horripilante. Escusado es decir que su querida, que es una *lúmia*, está en la galera, y su padre concluyó sus días á manos del verdugo de Valladolid, en cuyo canal dejó fama de hombre de *malas tripas y mu campechano*.

Cuando el buen Chato arma un escándalo en la *Casa de poco trigo*, y llega á entrar el alcaide para rejistrar á los presos y buscar las navajas, jamás se la encuentra, aunque le mande desnudar. Sábela esconder como ninguno, ya pegada con pez en la planta del pie, ya metida en el ano, burlando así la sagazidad del calabozero.

Los *barateros de playa*, si bien no tan desalmados como el Chato, son sin embargo de intenciones perversas, y suelen llegar á ser matones de las carceles y presidios; pues en realidad en nada se diferencian, siendo unas las costumbres y una la idea del *honor* que ellos se han formado, que tambien los barateros dicen que tienen *honor*, aunque para nosotros su honor vale tanto como el que sacan los ladrones de su villana profesion.

Agachados debajo de la proa de un falucho barado á la orilla de la mar en la playa de Málaga, se hallan cuatro ó seis charranes con sus cenachos al lado: una barajilla sucia y mugrienta, que por su estado pegajoso suelen llamarla allí de *arropiero*, y en Castilla de turronero, corre de mano en mano. El juego que los entretiene se llama ya el cané ó ya el *pecao*. En la arena hay algunos cuartos de los que *meten*. Su mirar es inquieto y zozobroso, porque temen la llegada repentina de un alguacil, que arrebañando *la mesa* consigue ademas cojer á alguno y dar con él en la carcel. Pero en los *alreores* no se dica

his head a handkerchief[36] that gives a sinister and horrifying aspect. Needless to say that his mistress, who is a prostitute, is in prison, and his father ended his days at the hands of the executioner of Valladolid, leaving in the gutter the reputation of man of cruelty and crudity.

When good Chato raises a scandal in the *Casa de poco trigo*, and the warden arrives to let in the prisoners and to search for *navajas*, never are they found, even if he sends them to undress. For they know how to hide things like no other, glued with pitch on the sole of the foot, already stuck in the anus, thus mocking the shrewdness of the *calabozero*.

The *barateros* of the beach, although not as heartless as Chato, are none the less of perverse intentions, and they come to be bullies in jails and garrisons; because in reality they are no different, coming from the customs and ideas of the honour that they have formed, also the *barateros* say that they have honour; although for us this honour is worth as much as that which the thieves take from their villainous profession.

Crouching under the prow of a small cheap fisherman's boat on the seashore at the beach of Málaga, there are four or six *charranes* with their fish baskets to the side: a dirty and greasy deck of cards, which due to its sticky state is often referred to as *'plates of arrope sweet cakes'*, and in Castilla, *'plates of "turron" candy'*[37], running from hand to hand. The game that entertains them is called already the *cané* or the *pecao*[38]. On the sand there are some *cuartos*[39] that they throw in. Their look is restless and anxious, because they fear the sudden arrival of a constable, who would clear the table and may succeed in catching some and sending them to jail. But there are none around,

ninguno, y juego continúa con sus blasfemias é interjecciones correspondientes.

De pronto y sin saber cómo, se asomó al corro una cabeza que llevaba calado un gorro encarnado algo descolorido: la cara de aquella cabeza era atezada, tenia unas patillas de *boca de jacha*, grandes y pobladas cejas. La susodicha cabeza pertenecía á un cuerpo alto, robusto, en cuya cintura se liaba una faja moruna, y de cuyo hombro izquierdo pendia una chaqueta forrada de bayeta encarnada; era un baratero.

- Ahí va eso, dijo el jaqueton tirando al corro una cosa liada en un papel de estraza en que antes se habia envuelto pescado frito; era una baraja.

Uno de los charranes le mira al rostro, recojé los naipes y se los devuelve al maton, diciéndole:

- Estimando, camará, nojotros no nesesitamos jeso.

- Chiquiyo, le repone el héroe del Perchél, venga aquí el barato, y… sonsoniche!

Los charranes recojen los chavos y se levantan mirando al *cobraor* con aquel aire pillesco y zumbon, propio de los de su clase. Al maton se le *ajuma el pescao*, alza la mano y *quié pegales*, pero uno de ellos da un salto atrás, desembucha una tea, y sin andarse en piquis miquis, zás! le pega un metio que da con el baratero en tierra.

Las olas del mar bañan á poco rato un cadaver…

Pero pasado unos dos meses, se oia por las calles de la poblacion una campanilla y la voz de un hombre que decia: "para hacer bien y decir misas por el alma de un pobre que van á ajusticiar."

and play continues with their blasphemies and inevitable interjections.

Suddenly and unexpectedly, a head is stuck into the circle wearing a somewhat faded red cap: the face of that head was dark, with *jacha* style sideburns[40], and large and bushy eyebrows. The aforementioned head belonged to a tall body, robust, on whose waist was tied a Moorish sash, and from whose left shoulder hung a jacket lined with red cloth; he was a *baratero*.

- Take this, says the braggart throwing into the circle something bundled in brown paper which before had been used to wrap fried fish; It was a card deck.

One of the rascals looks at the face, picks up the cards and he returns them to the thug, saying:

- Esteemed comrade, we don't need that.

- *Chiquiyo* [brat], responds that hero of *Perchél*[41], hurry here do the deal, and... get a move on! [42]

The rascals gather up the money and stand up looking at the *cobraor* with that air of grimace and mocking, typical of those of their class. The thug is incensed[43], raises his hands to give them a beating, but one of them jumps back, flicks out a knife, and without warning launches a sneaky attack, *zás!* [44] He strikes in a way that lands the *baratero* on the ground.

The waves of the sea soon bathe a corpse...

But after the passing of about two months, a bell is heard in the streets of the town and the voice of a man saying: "Do good and say Mass for the soul of a poor man who going to be executed."

A fin de perfeccionar el cuadro anterior, trasladamos aqui la linda composicion del distinguido poeta don Manuel Breton de los Herreros, titulada

EL BARATERO.

Al que me gruña le mato,
que yo compré la baraja
    ¿está osté?
Ya desnudé, mi navaja:
lárgue el coscon y el novato
    su parné,
porque yo cobro el barato
en las chapas y el cané.

Tiemblan sarjentos y cabos
cuando me pongo furioso:
    ¿está osté?
En donde yo campo y toso
no hay ternejales, no hay bravos,
    ¡chachipé!
porque yo cobro los chavos
en las chapas y el cané.

A naide temo ni envidio:
soy mu feroz y mu cruo:
    ¿está osté?
Y si la ley del embuo
me echa mañana á presidio,
    yo sabré
cobrar en Seuta el susidio
de las chapas y el cané.

In order to perfect the previous picture, we copy here the beautiful composition of the distinguished poet Don Manuel Breton de los Herreros, entitled

THE BARATERO[45].

I kill any who accuse me,
that I fixed the card deck[46]
  And you?
It is unsheathed, my *navaja*:
Scared from the crafty and the naive[47]
  his money,
because I charge[48] the *barato*
in the coins and the cards[49].

The sergeants and corporals tremble
when I get angry:
  And you?
Where I camp and cough[50]
there are no rogues, there are no bravos[51],
  Awesome! [52]
because I collect the money
in the coins and the cards.

No one do I fear or envy:
I am ferocious and severe:
  And you?
And if the law of the streets
throws me into jail tomorrow,
  I will know
To charge in Seuta[53] the earnings
of the coins and the cards.

Rico trujan y buen trago.....
¡Tengo una vida de obispo!
 ¿está osté?
Mi voluntá satisfago
y á costa ajena machispo,
 ¿y por qué?
Porque yo cobro y no pago
en las chapas y el cané.

 Así camelo y recluto
el corazon de mi mosa:
 ¿está osté?
Y aunque ha peinao corosa,
seré su rey asoluto:
 ¡lo seré!
mientras me paguen tributo
en las chapas y el cané.

Rich tobacco and good drink.....
I have a bishop's life!
      And you?
My will is satisfied
and to foreign coasts I escape,
      and why?
Because I charge and do not pay
in the coins and the cards.

   So I seduced and captured
the heart of my lass:
      And you?
She even grooms her head for a crown[54],
I will be her king absolute:
      I will be!
as long as they pay me tribute
in the coins and the cards.

APPENDIX: CONTEMPORARY SOURCES

Included are relevant sections from contemporary writings regarding 19th Century Spain and its culture. Excerpts are particularly of references to knives, *Baratero*, and *Jitanos*. These are provided to give the reader a deeper insight into the world of the *Baratero*; Spain in the mid to late 1800's.

L'ESPAGNE

First presented are sections from *L'Espagne* (1874, Paris) written by Baron Charles Davillier and illustrated by the famous artist Gustav Dore. Originally these were published in France as volumes of the periodical magazine *Voyages en Espagne* and later released as a complete book. The sections are English translations from the original French. There is an English version *Spain*, (1876, New York) by J Thomson FRGS, however this is not included as it is not a complete translation of the original and much less detailed.

Of note are portions of *L'espagne* that closely resemble the earlier *Manual del Baratero*, which in turn resemble words from Richard Ford's *Travellers Handbook*. The *Manual del Baratero* is referenced in *L'Espagne* and a part of the final poem is included.

Another point of interest is the section describing the experience of Davillier and Dore training with a knife master, and the similarity to other more recently published stories.

ZINCALI

Second are paragraphs from *Zincali: An Account of the Gypsies of Spain* (1841, London) written in English by George Borrow in two volumes and numerous editions printed. These books are mentioned by Davillier in *L'Espagne*, and give significant insight into the lives of the Spanish *gitanos* of the time. The sections included are specifically in reference to the use of the *tijeras*, scissors.

A TRAVELLER'S HANDBOOK

Third are extracts from *Handbook for Travellers in Spain* (1845, London) by Richard Ford, published by John Murray, who also publish George Borrow's *Zincali*. Ford presents, as with *L'Espagne*, a window into the social atmosphere and blade culture in Spain in the mid 1800's. There is also a great similarity in some sections to the later *Manual del Baratero* and *L'Espagne*.

Ford spent significant time travelling through Spain on horseback. He wrote an original version in 1844/45 but it was abandoned, unfinished, and unpublished. A version was released as two volumes (1845) and numerous reprints published as late as 1966. In 1846 the work was was edited and renamed 'Gatherings from Spain' in a single volume. Another single volume work, 'The Spaniards and their Country' was first published in 1848 and has many similarities to the original Handbook.

Of interest is an admonishment at the start of the book to Spanish innkeepers to not send false claims to be included in the travelogue:

"No attention can be paid to letters from innkeepers in praise of their own houses; and the postage of them is so onerous that they cannot be received." (Ford, 1845)

Another disclaimer that local information and recommendations, were gathered by personal experience rather than by other less trustworthy means (amusing in connection to the descriptions of the nature of the *Baratero* at the time):

"Caution to Innkeepers and others. — The Editor of the Hand-books has learned from various quarters that a person or persons have of late been extorting money from innkeepers, tradespeople, artists, and others, on the Continent, under pretext of procuring recommendations and favourable notices of them and their establishments in the Hand-books for Travellers.

The Editor, therefore, thinks proper to warn all whom it may concern, that recommendations in the Hand-books are not to be obtained by purchase, and that the persons alluded to are not only unauthorised by him, but are totally unknown to him. All those, therefore, who put confidence in such promises may rest assured that they will be defrauded of their money without attaining their object.— 1845." (Ford 1845)

LA NAVAJA.

Baron Charles Davillier (1874, Paris) *L'Espagne*
(translated from the original French)

[p100] Albacete is to Spain what Châtellerault is to France, Sheffield to England; the *navajas*, the *cuchillos*, the *puñales*, are manufactured there by the thousands: cutlery which can not be more coarse, and whose appearance is similar to that of Arabic works. The *navaja* is one of the *cosas de Espana*[55]; its form varies little; the neck, made of wood or horn, is covered with a copper plate adorned with some rudimentary engravings, and pierced here and there with a few holes under which shines the foil[56]. The blade, very elongated and pointed like a needle, is swollen in the middle, and is quite reminiscent of the shape of some fish: some grooves, hollowed parallel lengthwise are painted in the blood red of beef.

The blades of Albacete, of a very coarse iron, have nothing to do with those of Toledo; on the other hand, there are the most picturesque engraved inscriptions with etchings, and accompanied by arabesques of a style part oriental. Sometimes we read a motto borrowed from old Castilian arms, like this one, which does not lack a certain grandeur:

[p103] **KNIVES of ALBACETE**
"No me saques sin razon,
"No me embaines sin honor."
"Do not draw me for no reason, - Do not sheath me without honor. "

Quite often, the inscription contains a very uncomfortable threat for the opponent:
"Si esta vivora te pica,
"No hay remedio in the bótica."
"If this viper pricks you, - There is no cure at the pharmacy. "

It is undoubtedly this motto, used in preference to all the others, that has given to certain *navajas* the name of *navajas del santolio*, a mournful joke which means knives of extreme unction[57].

Sometimes the motto has only a purely defensive meaning:
« *Soy defensora de mi dueño solo, y viva!* » ["I am a defender of my owner alone, and alive!"]
Or even :
« *Soy defensa del honor de mi dueño.* » ["I defend the honour of my master."]

The *navajas* are ordinarily fitted with a very long iron spring; many notches at the heel of the blade strike the spring when you open the instrument, which produces a small harsh noise roughly similar to that made by a pistol that is armed, but much longer, since there are sometimes as many as twelve or fifteen notches on the great *navajas*: it is not uncommon to see those whose length exceeds one meter; it is true that these are only objects of pure fantasy, of which we do not make use; the length of ordinary *navajas* hardly exceeds a media vara [half yard], or about forty-five centimeters, which is already quite decent for a knife. The Spaniards pleasantly give them the name of *cortaplumas*, pocketknife, *mondadientes*, toothpick, or *alfiler*, which simply means a pin.

The art of handling *navaja* has its principles and rules, as does fencing, and there are well-known masters, mainly in Andalusia. One day we had the curiosity to take some lessons from a professor, a diestro; he showed us his art by means of a simple rush, which replaced for us the unbuttoned foil[58]. The main blow, the classic blow, consists in making on the face of the adversary one or two scars before striking him with a thrust from the bottom up: in this way, if one misses one's enemy, one has at least the consolation to paint him a *chebek, pintar a javeque*, an expression that probably comes from the fact that the scar is long and tapered like the sail of this Mediterranean boat [a small 3 masted boat]. It is not uncommon to see these scars on the faces of the *charranes* or *barateros*, people of the lowest class. When we arrive in Andalusia, we will have the opportunity to come back to this subject in more detail.

The Spanish *puñal* is much like the Corsican poignard (dagger): sometimes the blade is pierced through and made with small notches (serrated), a kindly precaution which aims to tear the wound, and make a more dangerous injury.

Here is a very serious question: do the Spanish (women) wear, according to the ancient reputation they have made, the dagger in the garter? We used to speak of *manolas* armed in this way, and they were even called *las del cuchillo en la liga*, literally: those with a knife in the garter. I have a small dagger very cute, a *puñalico*, which carries for motto:

« Sirvo á una dama : » [I serve a lady]

only the inscription is not explicit enough to teach us if the dagger was used by [p104] a lady for this use so interesting .... Let's hope, however, for the sake of the local colour!

[p126] The *gitanos* of today are far from being as formidable as those of the past: among the numerous faults they were accused of, only one remains, it is their inclination to theft; this tendency is general among *gitanos*, men or women, young or old, and it may be affirmed that the lines of Cervantes quoted a little above have remained true of every point. Apart from that, they are generally of inoffensive morals, and it is rather rare to see condemnation for murder; yet it is not without example that they have bloody quarrels between them; the cause is often jealousy, never theft; because the *gitanos*, who get along so well to steal from Christians - the *busnés*, as they call them in their jargon - never thieving among themselves.

Sometimes the formidable *navaja*, with a long blade and pointed like an aloe leaf, is their fighting weapon; but the *cachas*, long scissors which serve to cut the beasts of burden, are a still more terrible weapon, and only they [the gitanos] can handle with dexterity. There are scarcely any in Spain, from the Pyrenees to the Alpujarras, a horse, mule or donkey, which does not pass each year through the hands of a *gitano esquilador*

[farrier] or shearer: this industry seems to have been their exclusive privilege for several centuries, and among the Spaniards of old stock [ancestry], *cristianos viejos y rancios*[ancient Christians], as they like to call themselves, it would be difficult to find *esquiladors*, except in some parts of Aragon. The *gitanos* are the only ones who use this weapon of a new kind for the fight: as they carry almost always hanging on their belt the large kit which contains their *cachas* of different dimensions, they are not long to put themselves on guard in case of duel. The length of their scissors reach almost a foot and a half; only, instead of keeping them closed and using them as a *puñal* or a *navaja*, they hold them open, clasping them with their black and calming hands at the point of intersection of the two branches, so that one would think them armed with those old daggers whose blade would open in two at the press of a button.

Another trade of which the *gitanos* have a monopoly, is that of a horse dealer: there is no secret that they do not know, to give vigour to the weakest of horses [nags], or at least the appearance of vigour; we had, at the market at Totana, the opportunity of admiring their marvelous cleverness in this respect. As for women, they perform no other job than that of dancers and fortune-tellers: as soon as they behold a stranger, they go to him, take his hand, and, reading in the creases, they pronounce some unintelligible words with an inspired air, which usually earns them a few small coins.

Mr. George Borrow, the author of the curious book entitled The Zincali, is the one who has best studied the *gitanos*: we know he had the patience to learn their language, the *caló*, and he lived several years in the midst of them, hoping to convert them to Protestantism; he relates that one day, having a mule loaded with Bibles, a *gitano* took his load for soap packets: "Yes," he replied, "it's soap, but soap to clean souls! This missionary ended up pretending to be one of them, but those who know them well can hardly believe that he has made many proselytes among them.

MALAGA.

We found the quays of Malaga cluttered with boxes of *pasas* and barrels of all sizes. The wines and *pasas* -so-called *raisins* - are the principal productions of Malaga; however, let us not forget the coloured terracotta industry; it is in the Pasaje de Heredia that these statuettes are modelled, which invariably represent Andalusian costumes: sometimes it is a *maja* with a short petticoat, dancing *polo* or *jaleo*; sometimes it is a *contrabandista*, the *trabuco* in the hand; a cutting *majo*, with his *navaja*, the tobacco destined for his cigarette, or a priest with the long hat, *sombrero de teja*.

If the use of *navaja*, *puñal* and *cuchillo* is general in Spain, there are certain cities where the healthy traditions are preserved more particularly; Cordova and Seville have well-known masters; but nowhere is the art of handling iron - the *herramienta* - cultivated as much as in Malaga. Few cities offer the example of such a homicidal inclination, and it is said that there is scarcely any place where *delitos de sangre* - the crimes of blood - are so frequent. From where does this habit of murder come, so general among the people? Is it idleness, the passion of gambling, or the negligence of the police? "The *serenos* of Malaga," said a popular chorus « pretend they do not drink wine; but the wine they drink would be enough to turn a mill: »

En Mâlaga los serenos	In Mâlaga the serenos
Dicen que no beben vino;	They say they do not drink wine;
Y con elvino que beben,	And with the wine they drink,
Puede moler un molino!	You can grind a mill!

Must we still attribute, as has been claimed, the bloody issue of the quarrels of a certain class to the *solano*, to this burning wind coming from Africa, impregnated, like the sirocco of the *Napolitains*, with the irritating heat of the sands of the Sahara? Be that as it may, the impunity of the assassins is proverbial: *Mata al rey, y vete á Málaga*, - Kill the king, and go to Malaga; - as is the popular saying.

Already, speaking of Albacete, we have cited this city as very famous for the manufacture of *navajas*; Guadiz, Seville, Mora, Valencia, Jaen, Santa Cruz de Mudela, and other cities also have famous cutlers. Besides many other fancy names that the *navaja* receives, it is still called, in Andalusia, the *mojosa*, the *chaira*, the *tea*, expressions more particular to the *gitanos*; the *barateros*, of whom we shall speak soon, call it rather *corte* (sharp), *herramienta* or *hierro* (iron), *abanico* (fan), etc.

During our stay in Malaga, we had the fancy to take lessons from one of the [p246] professors of reputation: after a few sessions, Doré had become a distinguished student; armed with small canes [sticks] carved into n*avaja*, we engaged in harsh assaults, and we wore, according to all the rules of a special fencing, the most terrible blows of edge and point [cut and thrust]: the thumb placed on the widest part of the blade, the left hand fixed against the waist, the legs slightly open, in order to make the changes easier, that was our position when we prepared ourselves to slaughter each other. The professor then began the demonstration of the different *golpes*, - that is what we call blows, - who also receive the name of *puñaladas*, or *puñalas*, according to the Andalusian pronunciation. These blows are struck in the *parte alta* [high part] or in the *parte baja* [low part]: the upper part extends from the top of the head to the waist, and the lower part from the waist to the feet, such that the blows are *altos* or *bajos*, depending on whether they are given in the upper or lower part of the body.

One of the main strokes of the high part is the *javeque* or *chirlo*: thus is named a large slash made in the face with the sharpness of the *navaja*, and which elongates like the tapered sail of the *javeque*; the *javeque* is regarded, by the *barateros*, as an ignominious wound, because of all the blows one may receive, it is the one which best shows the wounded man's clumsiness [lack of skill], and the disregard that the diestro – the skillful – makes of his opponent, by being content to simply mark him instead of killing him. Another stroke of the parte alta, a blow infinitely more serious, and which demands a great skill, is the *desjarretazo*; It is given from behind, above the last rib: the *desjarretazo* is a blow very esteemed,

not by the one who receives it, of course, because it is almost always mortal, especially when the blade, opening a wide injury, separates the spine in two. Only, since nothing in the world is perfect, this pretty blow has the disadvantage of uncovering the diestro who gives it, and to expose him to receive at the same time a blow of the point in the belly.

[p247] L' ESCRIME A LA NAVAJA

Let us also mention the *plumada*, a blow that is given from right to left by describing a curve, and the *revés*, carried from left to right, with the arm extended and suddenly brought back; the *culebra*, which consists in quickly throwing one's face to the ground, leaning on one's left hand, and striking upwards, with the other hand, a blow in the lower abdomen; the *floretazo*, used against the adversary who advances too quickly, and who comes himself to be stuck upon the tip of the *navaja*: by giving a *floretazo*, you would run high risk of being hurt yourself, if the body was not thrown back.

The *tiradores*, or experienced fighters, still recommend the *corrida* as one of the most useful blows to know: the *corrida*, which requires a particular lightness and a lot of cold blood, is executed by making a rapid oblique movement to the right or to the left, in order to hit the opponent in the side. The *golpes de costado* are not less dangerous: they are the blows which are given between the ribs, and it is rare that they are not mortal.

UN DUELO A LA NAVAJA DEL SANTOLIO.

Sometimes the *tiradores* place on their left arm their *manta*, or their wrapped jacket, like the *giuoco della spada e cappa* [plays of the sword and cloak] represented by ancient Italian fencing books; or they hold in their hand their *sombrero*, which they use as a shield. These means of defence are very much discussed: the principal reproach that the purists respond to this, it prevents the use of the left hand; for any accomplished *tirador* must know how to handle his weapon indistinctly with both hands. As for the *faja*, or belt, the *navaja* fighters never fail to gird their kidneys [surround their sides], for it is of great use for the defence; only is it essential to fix it securely. If the belt were to be unraveled, the *tirador* would expose his feet being caught on the folds and falling; he would then run the greatest danger, for his adversary would not fail to profit by his fall.

Each blow, naturally, has its parries or *recursos*; There are different kinds of them: first, the *engaños* or *finjimientos* (feints), then the *tretas* or secret strikes; the latter are somewhat different from the rules of fencing as we understand it; for example, one throws the *sombrero* in the face of his adversary: it is a strike which rarely fails its effect; or the diestro bends down quickly to pick up a handful of sand with his left hand, which he throws in the eyes of his enemy, while with the other hand he strikes him in the belly. Sometimes one treads strongly on the feet of the adversary, he is heel kicked in the lower part of the abdomen, or one tries to make him fall by means of a *croc-en-jambe* [a leg hook]; or else one pretends to speak to an imaginary person who suddenly appears, to strike the *contrario* at the moment when he turns his head away, which is reminiscent of the famous *Coup du Commandeur*[59] of a certain room of the Palais-Royal.

Like the *navaja*, the *puñal* has its own fencing and its particular rules; this weapon, which is preferred by sailors and prisoners, is distinguished mainly from the *navaja* in that it is only used for thrusts, for the dagger hardly has any edge; ordinarily the handle, large and short, a little similar to the shape of an egg; as for the blade, it is sometimes flat and oval, sometimes round, sometimes four-sided; we brought from Malaga a

L'ESCRIME AU COUTEAU : LANZAR LA NAVAJA.

puñal which had belonged to one of the most formidable *barateros* of Perchel; this weapon, tapered and pointed like a needle, is something frightening: quadrangular on the side of the point, it then rounds imperceptibly; moreover, it is furnished with barbed notches, and the blade is pierced [with holes] in several places: ingenious precautions which have the double advantage of tearing the wound, and rendering it more dangerous by introducing air into it.

One of the main blows of the *puñal* is the *molinete*, of which Doré made a very exact drawing: one of the adversaries pivots rapidly on one foot, and raises his arm to wound his enemy behind the shoulder [a desjarretazo], who he has approached unexpectedly; he can only defend himself by trying to stop with his left hand the arm raised to strike him, and to strike at the same time with his right hand. It [p248] usually follows a hand-to-hand struggle, which almost always has a fatal result for the two combatants.

A curious little treatise, the *Manual del baratero* or *Arte de manejar la navaja*, also tells us how to throw this weapon, as well as the *puñal*: the handle of the weapon must be placed in the palm of the hand; the tip, turned inwards, turns towards the opponent at the moment when the diestro throws it by extending his hand with force. Sailors, who are used to wearing the *herramienta* attached to their belt by means of a long cord or a small chain of copper, are very practiced in *lanzar la navaja*. « Our readers, says our Andalusian [the author of MdB], will find it difficult to imagine the extraordinary precision with which we saw the *navaja* thrown, which was nailed in the chest or in the belly of the adversary, at the same place as the diestro had chosen; but what is no less surprising, is the particular skill with which some

Andalusians know how to avoid the blow; we have even seen some who were skillful enough to seize the cord which held the *navaja* of the *contrario*, and cut it with their own *navaja*. "

We have already spoken of the *tijeras*, those enormous scissors, of which the *esquiladores*, mostly *gitanos*, use with so much skill. These *tijeras* become in their hands a terrible weapon: the double wound caused by the two points is always dangerous, and sometimes mortal. Moreover, the fighting at the *tijera* is quite rare, the *gitanos* being of an essentially peaceful nature, and most of them have a horror of blood shed.

After having outlined the principle rules of a fencing peculiar to the Andalusians, we will say some words of two purely *malagueños* types: the *barateros* and the *charranes*, people of a particular skill to handle the *puñal* and the *navaja*.

[p251] LES CHARRANES

Tourists who spend some time in Malaga can study, if they do not fear certain people, extremely curious types, such as *charran* and *baratero*.

What is the *charran*? The Diccionario of the Spanish Academia does not teach us anything about this subject, and this word is also absent from other Spanish dictionaries. He is neither the boy of Paris nor the pale thug; he is not the Neapolitan *lazzarone*, and yet he is a little bit of all these. Let's go for a stroll in the *barrio del Perchel*, a district where fishermen spread their nets on *perchas* [hangers] to dry them; it is the rendezvous of *majos* [the trendy good looking people], as in Seville it is *la Macarena*; in Malaga, when one wishes to speak of a girl of the elegant and overflowing people, one says a Perchelera moza [girl], as in Seville they say a hembra [female] Macarena.

Let us approach this boat washed up on the beach, and in the shade of which men of the people are sitting and playing cards: they are *charranes*: they are born in Malaga, and they will die there, unless they do not finish their days at the presidio of Ceuta[60] or Melilla; they practise, it is true, an

apparent industry: thus they go through the streets selling *boquerones*. the local sardines; or they offer their services to the housewives who come to buy at the market the supply of the day; but their true state, is to do nothing, to live by industry in the bad sense of the word, to take the sun on the beach or the shadow on the esplanade of the wharf.

The *charran* is a boy of fourteen to twenty years; young, he is called *pillo*, a word roughly synonymous with thug; he is still called *granuja*, local expression which means grape seed and which entails an intention of contempt. The boys of Malaga have nothing to envy, in terms of skill, to the most skillful villains of Naples or London; we have personally experienced this, cheaply indeed, since it only cost us a handkerchief. They are very inventive in appropriating the property of others; we can judge by this little local history, which we report in all its purity, according to a *Malagueno* [resident of Malaga], it was a question of stealing from a brave *arriero*, descended from the mountain, an ounce of gold which he had put in his mouth, in the fear of the rogues. One Sunday, our *arriero* met at the Puerta de Mar a peasant friend, who urged him to accompany him to the church; the suspicious mountaineer refused, saying that he had an ounce of gold in his *faja*, and that he feared to be in the midst of the crowd. The peasant insisted, making the observation that this was not sufficient reason to miss Mass, - *perder la misa*; - and then, he added, put the ounce in your mouth: it will be safer than in your belt.

This reason appeared conclusive to the *arriero*, who with his friend took the way to the church. Some scoundrels, *pillos*, *granujas*, or *charranes*, had heard the conversation, and had seen the ounce of gold pass from the *faja* into the mouth of the *arriero*; three of them detached themselves from their comrades, and followed their victim into the church. Before entering, they each took the two corners of a handkerchief into which they threw a few small coins, and began to play naturally the role of two sailors asking for offerings to say mass to the Vierge del Cármen [the Virgin of Cármen]. They thus approached the *arriero*, who was standing in the middle of a group, clenching his teeth to better guard his ounce,

CHALOUPES ET MATELOTS SUR LA PLAGE (page 251)

and looking sideways at all those who were around him; the false sailors had knelt down, and pretended to murmur prayers, without losing sight of the *arriero*. Finally, after the "*Ite missa est*" [61], one of them suddenly dropped the corners of the handkerchief, and the coins rolled on the flagstones. «Caballeros, nobody move," cried one of the *charranes*, "all this money belongs to the [p252] Virjen Santisima! [Holy Virgin] Look out for the ounce! Where is the ounce of gold?» All the attendants bent down to look, except for the fake sailors, who resumed aloud: «Nobody has seen the ounce for the mass of *Maria Santisima*? Who took the ounce?

«It is this rascal who has just picked it up and put it in his mouth," cried one of the assistants, who was none other than a friend [of the *charranes*], pointing at the poor *arriero*. The latter, confused and caught, naively brought his hand to his mouth, and withdrew the ounce of gold, which one of the assistants, - always a friend, - snatched violently from his hands with well played indignation, and put it back in the handkerchief of the poor sailors. The public, indignant, - overwhelmed the so-called thief with reproaches, and when he was finally able to open the mouth to protest his innocence, the *charranes*, who had slipped through the crowd like serpents through a bush, shared the ounce of gold outside the church.

Despite their dilapidated costume, these *lazzaroni* from Malaga have a certain casualness that prevents them from being confused with beggars by profession; for the rest they do not ask: they like to fly better; the *esplanade del Muelle* is the ordinary theatre of their exploits; it is there that they are in the habit of levying tithes on the goods they are selling; sometimes it is a *bacalao* [cod] that they adroitly pass under their shirt, sometimes it is a huge onion, a melon, or some potatoes; they are still very adept at plunging their *navaja* into a bundle, to receive in their *sombrero* the rice that escapes from it, then they rendezvous in the dry bed of the torrent of Guadalmedina[62], or in some other remote place, where they cook between two stones, in some old shards [old pottery], the products of their marauding.

LE CHARRAN DE MALAGA.

It is rare that these feasts do not end with a game of cards, because they are great gamblers, like almost all the Andalusians of the lower class: a filthy mantle, folded in four and thrown on the ground, serves them as a playing mat; the cards are so worn from use that it is hardly possible to distinguish the points. They are no less passionate about games of chance, especially that of head or tails [coins], - *cara y cruz* [63]; - and as they do not fail to cheat, it is rare that the game ends without some fight, where the blows fists, sticks and stones rain like hail; the *pedreas*, so they call their fights with stones, usually take place in the torrent of Guadalmedina, which provides them with projectiles of any calibre. This is also where the quarrels [p253] of *barrios* are emptied, for there are in Malaga three *barrios* or rival districts: Victoria, Perchel and Trinidad, whose inhabitants have mores [traditions] and even particular costumes. It is in vain that the authorities wanted to stop the *pedreas*, which are renewed from time to time, especially on Sundays and holidays.

The *charran* is a big smoker, and a master at picking up cigar ends, which he immediately turns into cigarettes. When chance has brought a *puro* [a pure unsmoked full cigar/cigarette] into his hands, he shares it fraternally with his comrades: this sharing takes place in a rather original way: the rascals are placed by age, and in a circle: the oldest ignites the cigar takes a whiff of breath [inhale], and passes it to his neighbour, who does the same; and the *puro* passes from hand to hand, each one inhaling the largest possible *chupada* [drag/puff], until it is completely extinguished.

The *charran* sleep summer under the stars, along the houses, without worrying about mosquitoes, whose tanned skin defies stings. In winter, he always finds a *zaguan* or portico to rest his head sheltered from the north winds. Although he is involved in all the demonstrations and he is in all the riots, he has no political opinion: it is said that when the French troops, under the orders of General Sebastiani, presented themselves in front of Malaga, groups of *charranes* mingled with the partisans of the resistance, uttering cries of: Viva Ferdinando VII!
People armed with knives and daggers could not hold out long before the grape shot, and the French were not long in making their entry into the

city, preceded by the same groups, who shouted at the top of their voices: Viva Napoleon!

We have already said a few words about the *baratero*: he is a man of the dregs of the people, who has acquired an extraordinary ability to handle *navaja* and *puñal*, and who exploits the terror he inspires to demand of the players a right [commission] on the stake of the game. As we have already said, the lower-class Andalusians are extreme gamblers: each city contains a certain number of people without profession called *tahures,* which corresponds roughly to that of *grecs* [64], and who have no other industry than the game [gambling].

It is rare that the vices of a nation are not many times the secular: the orders of Alphonse the Savant against the *tafurerias* or gambling houses prove that from that time the passion of gambling was already very violent in Spain; it had not diminished in the seventeenth century, if we believe a curious work of a Sevillian author, the licensee Fajardo, against idlers and gamblers, a work in which the author lists the numerous tricks, practices and scams used by the *grecs* of the time.

Each city of Andalusia has its *garitos* or gambling dens, where professional players meet, to whom one could still apply these old verses:

Ya el jugador de España
Su esperanza no fía
En el incierto azar, sino en la maña.

Already the player of Spain
Your hope does not trust
In uncertain chance, but in skill.

«Today, the Spanish player does not put his hope in the uncertain chance, but in the skill of his fingers. »

The *garitos* are not the only places for the players; they meet everywhere: on the beach, in the shadow of a boat; under the trees of a promenade, or sheltered from an old wall, in some remote place: the audience is usually composed of *charranes* and other people without profession, in which some sailors and some soldiers mingle. See them along this *falucho* [a small boat with oars and a lateen sail] [254] stranded on the sand, and whose sails dry in the sun: some are seated, the others lie on their stomachs in front of a dirty card game; they play cané, or *pecao*, or some other of their favourite games; their body language is restless and agitated, either by the passion of the game or by the fear to see an *alguacil* [constable] arrive.

Suddenly, and without anyone knowing where he came from, an individual with a pale complexion and a sinister face, with a bold and provocative air, appears in the middle of the group: he is a robust man, *bien empatillado*, that is, adorned with a large pair of side-burns; he wears his jacket over his shoulder, and his short trousers are held in place by a wide silk belt: he is a *baratero*, who settles without a care side by side with the players, and announces to them brusquely that he comes to take his share of the stake, -*cobrar el barato;*- that is what is called the type of tribute which he claims for himself the right to levy, and which, moreover, ordinarily consists only of a very small sum; two or three *cuartos* at most, or about ten centimes per game.

«*Ahi va eso!* [There goes that!] exclaims the *baratero* throwing an object into the middle of the group, surrounded by an old grey paper which must have been used to wrap fried fish: it is a pack of old cards, - *baraja,* - which signifies that you don't have to play with your cards: *Aqui no se juega sino con mis barajas!* «Here, we only play with my cards!» If the players are of good disposition, the *baratero* pockets his *cuartos*, and everything goes peacefully. But it happens sometimes that there is in the group a *valiente*, - a brave man, -a *mozo cruo*, literally: a raw boy, an Andalusian expression almost untranslatable, which means a bold and brave young man. This one answers without fear, with a strong Andalusian accent: *Camará, nojotros no necesitamos jeso!* - «Comrade,

we do not need them!» And he returns the playing cards to the *baratero*. «*Chiquiyo*, take this one, *venga aqui el barato, y sonsoniche!* «Kid, pass me the *barato* quickly, and not a word!» The *mozo cruo* then pulls a long knife attached to his belt, opens it with the clicking of the springs, pushes the point next to the stake, and exclaims whilst looking with an air of defiance at the provocateur: *Aquí no se cobra el barato sino con la punta de una navaja!* «Here we only touch the *barato* with the point of a *navaja*.»

It is rare that the challenge is not accepted; in this case the two adversaries pronounce the solemn *vamonos!* or *vamos alli*! «Let's go!» or even: *Vamos de una viaje!* «Let's go for a trip!» It's their *alea jacta est* [the die is cast]. They go into a remote corner, the *navajas* or *puñales* are pulled from the belts and shine in the air, and one of the adversaries falls bleeding.

Murder does not always go unpunished, and sometimes two or three months later the streets of the city can be heard as the sound of a small bell and the voice of a man asking for alms *para decir misas por el alma de un pobre que van d ajusticiar*, «to say Mass for the soul of an unfortunate man who will be judged.»

It also happens that two *barateros* meet on the same ground, and that the newcomer claims his share of the stake; sometimes the quarrel ends with a duel to the death; we have seen them caught up in a narrow courtyard and strike at each other with knives until one of them falls inanimate. But sometimes also these adversaries have only the appearance of bravery and realise this type of killing bravado, daring with the weak, quietly disappears when one stands up to him: a type known as *maton, matachin, valenton, perdonavidas, e*tc [thug, bully, braggart]. When two brave men of this species have an interaction, a most amusing dialogue is established between them, of which we will try to give an idea, although the Andalusian dialect loses, in passing to another language, a lot of its originality.

«*Ea!* it is here that the brave men will show themselves, says one of them, making the springs of his *navaja cry out!*
- *Tire oste!* Draw! comrade Juan, exclaims the other, turning around his opponent.
- *Vente di mi, Curriyo!* [Come at me!] not so many turns and detours!

LES BARATEROS

- It's you, zeño Juan, who jump like a little dog.
- *Ea, Dios mio!* Here, you can recommend your soul to God!
- Did I wound you?
- No it is nothing!
- Well! I will kill you at once; you can ask for extreme unction.
- Save yourself, *por Dios, Curriyo*, you see that I have the upper hand, and I'll open you a wound bigger than the arch of a bridge. "

This dialogue would continue for more than an hour, if friends did not intervene; the two adversaries, who ask nothing better than to appease themselves, close their knives, and they go to some *taberna*, where they forget the quarrel by emptying some *cañas de jerez* [cups of wine].

In addition to the *barateros de playa*, who practice on the beach, there is also that of the *cárcel*, who reigns in the prison, and the *baratero soldado* or *tropa* [soldiers or troops]: the latter is the tyrant of the company or the regiment; the sergeant, who does not wish to have him for an enemy, exempts him from chores; there is no quarrel with which he is not mixed up; he scarcely knows the elements of the exercise, and he professes the greatest repugnance for discipline; for example, he is of the best strength in the handling of the knife. The *baratero soldado* does not refuse any enjoyment: he drinks the best, which the *cantiniere* pays him, and smokes *puros*; all this is paid for by the *barato* which he takes from the other soldiers. When the regiment is on march he receives the visit of comrades or compatriots - *camardas, compares* - from the locality where they halt; for there is between them a certain freemasonry, as between the Neapolitan *Camorristi*; they find themselves in *garitos* frequented by their *confrères* [brothers]. Sometimes however these interviews end in

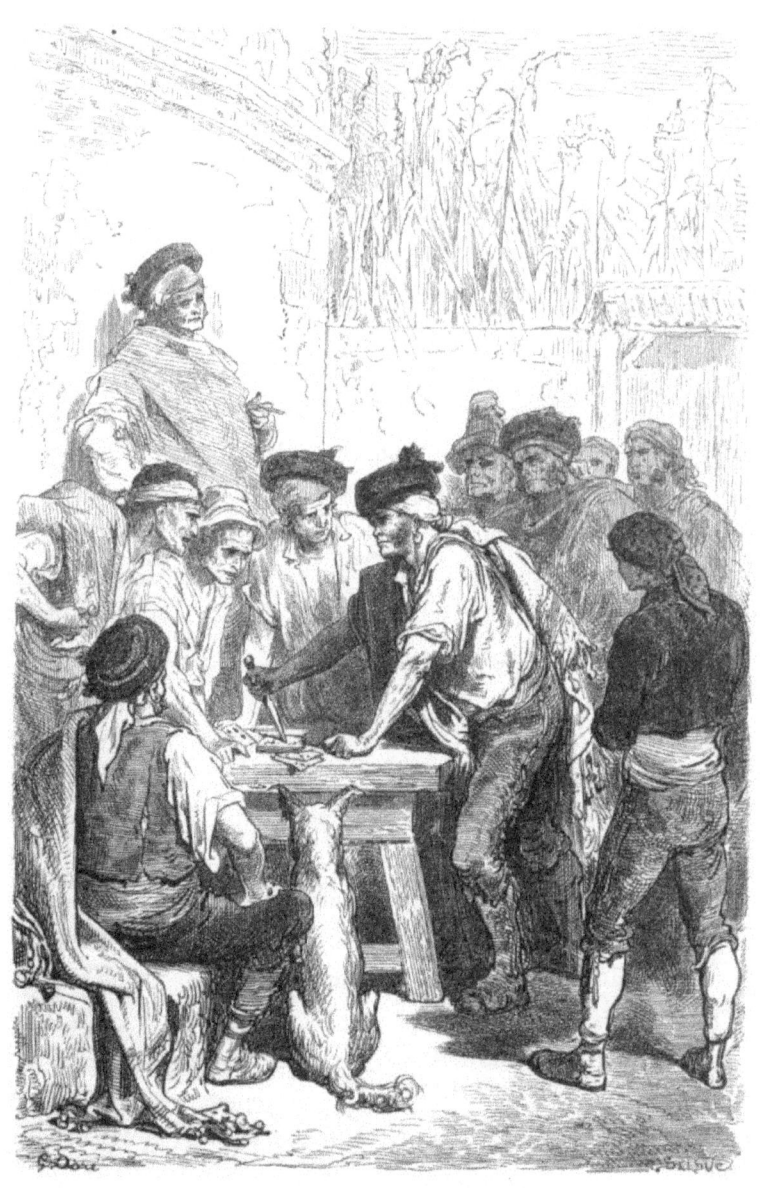

LE BARATERO EXIGEANT LE BARATO (page 254).

some *pendencia* [brawl], or quarrel: at the least contradiction, one throws at the other's face the *cañas de jerez*, container and contents, and they go out into the street to strike two or three *mojadas* [wet (bleeding) blows], after which they are better friends than before.

The *baratero de la carcel* is the most dangerous and the most odious of all; lost in vices from his childhood, he spent most of his existence in prison, - the *estarivél*, or *casa de poco trigo*, - literally the house where there is little wheat, as the thieves say in their picturesque slang. As soon as a freshly condemned prisoner has crossed the threshold of the prison, the *baratero* demands from him the *diesmo* [tithe], - the welcome. This demand is always made with *navaja* in hand, and if the new refuses to pay the *moneas*, the *metales*, the question is decided by means of some *navajasos* exchanged. When the law - in slang *severa* [the hard-faced] - intervenes to stop the killing, it is rare for the *navajas* to be found again; because the *carceleros* [prisoners] have all manner of means, each more ingenious than the other, to make them [the *navaja*] disappear.

L'ESCRIME AU PUÑAL : EL MOLINETTE (page 247).

To finish painting the strange image that we have just sketched, we will give some verses of an Andalusian song: El baratero, in *germania* or slang of the Spanish thieves:

Al que me gruña le mato,	Whoever whispers, I kill him,
Que yo compré la baraja.	Because I take the *baraja*;
Estâ osté?	Do you understand?
Ya desnudé mi navaja:	I just pulled my *navaja*:
Largue el coscon y el novato	Give, innocents and novices,
Su parné,	Your money:
Porque yo cobro el barato	It's me who touches the barato
En las chapas y en el cané.	At coins and cups
Rico trujan y bucn trago...	What rich tobacco! what good wine!
Tengo una vida de obispo !	I lead the life of bishop!
Estât osté?	Do you understand?
Mi voluntad satisfago	I satisfy all my tastes,
Y â costa ajena machispo,	And I live at the expense of others;
Y porque?	And why?
Porque yo cobroy no pago	Because I receive without paying,
En las chapas y en el cané.	At coins and cups[65].

[258] One can guess how the *baratero* usually end up: it is in a public square, or where a scaffold made of planks has been erected for the execution of the garrote; the executioner, after having passed around his neck the fatal collar of iron, the necktie of Vizcaya ", tightens the fatal screw while asking him the traditional forgiveness: *me perdonas?* "Literally the Biscay tie is the name given by thieves to the garrote, Biscay has long been famous for the work of iron.

George Borrow (1841, London)
Zincali: An Account of the gypsies of Spain

[p129] "...and then we defend ourselves as well as we can. There is no better weapon in the hands of a *Gitáno* than his *cachas*, or shears with which he trims the mules. I once snipped off the nose of a *Busnó* and opened the greater part of his cheek in an affray up the country near Trujillo."

[p143] The *esquilador* when proceeding to the exercise of his vocation, generally carries under his arm a small box, containing the instruments necessary, and which consist principally of various pairs of scissors, and the *aciál*, two short sticks tied together with whipcord at the end, by means of which the lower lip of the horse, should he prove restive, is twisted, and the animal reduced to speedy subjection. In the girdle of the *esquilador* are stuck the large scissors called in Spanish *tijeras* and in the Gypsy tongue *cachas* with which he principally works.

[p145] The *Gitänos* are in general very expert in the use of the *cachas*, which they handle in a manner practised nowhere but in Spain; and with this instrument the poorer class principally obtain their bread.

Richard Ford (1845, New York) *A Handbook for Travellers in Spain* Volume 1

[33]The luggage is piled up behind, or stowed away in a front boot. The management of driving this vehicle is conducted by two persons. The master *calesero* [carriage driver] is called the "*mayoral*", his helper or cad the "*mozo*" or, more properly, "*el zagal*," from the Arabic, a strong active youth. The costume of the *calesero* is peculiar, and is based on that of Andalucia, which sets the fashion all over the Peninsula, in all matters regarding bull-fighting, horse-dealing, and so forth. He wears on his head a gay-coloured silk handkerchief, tied in such a manner that the tails hang down behind; over this remnant of the Moorish turban, he wears a high-peaked sugarloaf-shaped hat, "*sombrero calanes*" with broad brims, "*gacho*" Arabice "turned down;" his jacket is the national "*jaqueta*" which is made either of black sheepskin, "*zamarra,*" studded with silver tags, "*alamares,*" and filigree buttons; or of brown cloth, with the back, arms, and particularly the [34] elbows, welted and tricked out with flowers and vases, cut in patches of different coloured cloth and much embroidered. These *calesero* jackets are often imitated by the dandies, the "*majos*" of whom more anon, and then they are called a "*marselles*" not from the French Marseilles, but from the old Moorish costume of Marsilla in Africa. In warm weather linen jackets are substituted. When the jacket is not worn it is usually hung over the left shoulder, after the hussar fashion. The waistcoat, "*chaleco,*" is made of rich fancy silk; the breeches, "*calzones*" are made of blue or green velvet plush, ornamented with stripes and filigree buttons, or fitting tight, "*de punto*" and tied at the knee with silken cords and tassels; the neck is left open, and the shirt-collar turned down, a gaudy neck-handkerchief is worn, oftener passed through a ring than tied in a knot; his waist is girt with a red sash, or with one of a bright yellow, "*color de caña.*" This "*faja*"* is a *sine quâ non*; it is the old Roman zona, it serves also for a purse; it "girds the loins" and keeps up a warmth over the abdomen, which is highly beneficial in hot climates, and wards off any tendency to irritable colic: in the sash is stuck the "*navaja,*" the knife, which is part and parcel of a Spaniard; behind, in the sash, the "*zagal*" usually places

his stick, "*la vara.*" The Andalucian *calesero* wears richly-embroidered gaiters, "*botines,*" ** which are left open at the outside to show a handsome stocking; the shoes are yellow, like those of our cricketers, "*de becerro*" of untanned calfskin. The *caleseros* on the eastern coast wear the Valencian stocking, which has no feet, and the ancient Roman sandals, made of the *esparto* rush, with hempen soles,"*alpargatas,*" Arabicé *Alpalgah.* The "*zagal*" follows the fashion in dress of the "*mayoral*" as nearly as his means will permit him.

*Faja ; the Hhezum of Cairo. Atrides tightens his sash when preparing for action- Iliad xi. 15. The Roman soldiers kept their money in it. Ibit qui *zonam* perdidit — Hor. ii. Ep. 2. 40. The Jews used it for the same purpose — Matthew x. 9; Mark vi. 8. It is loosened at night. " None shall slumber or sleep, neither shall the girdle of their loius [loins] be loosed."— Isaiah v. 27.

** The old leggings of the Iberians, χγημιδας— Strabo, iii. 232. Sometimes the hair was left on the leather, τριχιγας χγημιδας— Diod. Sic. v. 310.

[44] This mode, when the party is small, or when a person is alone, is very common in Spain; it is, perhaps, the cheapest and safest manner. The "*ordinarios*" who go from town to town, frequently compound with regularly established bands of robbers, by paying a certain black-mail, which secures their safe passage. They always travel in such numbers, and take such precautions, that nothing is to be apprehended from "*rateros*" or minor robbers. These muleteers, "*arrieros,*" are, moreover, the best persons to consult as to the actual condition of roads and those particulars which, changing from day to day, cannot be laid down in a book.

[44] The mules in Spain, as in the East, have their coats closely shorn or clipped; part of the hair is usually left on in stripes like the zebra, or cut into fanciful patterns, like the tattooings of an Indian chief. This process of shearing is found to keep the beast cooler and freer from cutaneous

disorders. The operation is performed in the southern provinces by gipsies, "*gitanos*" who are the same tinkers, horse-dealers, and vagrants in Spain as elsewhere. In the northern provinces all this is done by Arragonese, who, in costume, good-for-nothingness, and most respects, are no better than the worst real gipsies. This clipping recalls to us the "mulo curto," on which Horace could amble even to Brundusium.

[45] The mule-clippers are called "*esquiladores:*" they may be known by the formidable shears, *tijeras*, gipsicé [in gypsy language] "*cachas*" which they carry in their sashes. They are very particular in clipping the pastern and heels, which they say ought to be as free from hair as the palm of a lady's hand.

[83] To speak Spanish, and indeed any foreign language, well, a man must be a bit of a mimic as well as a linguist. He must have a quick eye and ear, and suit his action to his words; especially in Andalucia and southern countries, where bodily excitement keeps pace with mental imagination. It is no *still* life, and, although a pantomime, is anything but a dumb show: gesticulation is the safety-valve of the superabundant energy and caloric of the South. The most amicable discussion is conducted like a mortal fray, a logomachy, a *guerra al cuchillo*, or war to the knife—when compared to the quiet phlegm with which the most important affairs are debated in England. There is more row aboard a Spanish fishing-smack than an English line-of-battle ship: no man knows what conversational noise is till he has stepped from the steamer at once into the *Plaza de Cadiz*; it is *mucho ruido y pocas nueces*, much cry and little wool. Even the Spaniards feel that, and say that three women and two geese constitute a complete market —*ires mugeres con dos ganzos, hacen un mercado entero*. As far as power over, stress, intonation, and modulation (forgive the word) of the voice is concerned, even a Parisian might take a lesson on gesticulation. The traveller must reckon his shoulders and ten fingers among his parts of speech: without a little of this lively articulation they hardly think that you are serious.

[104] The sword and lance, the weapons of the Iberians, which were dearer to them than life itself, continued down to the 17th century to be the national defence: now the gun and knife have replaced them. It is reasonable to suppose that Spaniards, from always having these weapons in their hands, know how to use them; hence the facility with which what is here called an army is got together.

[147 Andalucia] No tailor nor hand-book can, however, make a *majo*, nor let any stranger venture too soon to play these frisks and gambols. Those who can, and do it well, become the envy and admiration of the *Plaza, que saleroso, que gracioso, que travesura que trastienda! que caidas tiene, que occurencias, derrama sal y canela, y es la sal de las sales* [the charmer, the fool, the cunning mischief! the falls, the situations, spilling salt and cinnamon, the salt of the salts]. The *Majo* of the lower classes often degenerates into a Bravo, a bully, a fire-eater, and flashman, *muy guapo, y valiente*. He is the *Baratero*, who levies forfeit-money from all who will not fight him. Such are the natives of Andalucia.

[200] The *capa* is shaped in a peculiar manner, and is rounded at the bottom; the circumference of the real and correct thing is seven yards all but three inches and a half: "*bis ter ulnarum toga.*" As cloaks, like coats, are cut according to a man's cloth, a scanty *capa*, like the "*toga arcta*" of Horace, does not indicate affluence, or even respectability. Sn Isidoro did well to teach his Goths that their *toga* was a *tegendo*, because it concealed the whole man, as it does now, provided it be a good one, *una buena capa, todo tapa*. It covers a multitude of sins, and especially pride and poverty, twin sisters in Iberia, The ample folds and graceful drapery give breadth and throw an air of stately decency —nay, dignity —over the wearer; it not only conceals tatters and nakedness, but appears to us to invest the pauper with the abstract classicality of an ancient peripatetic philosopher, since we never see this costume of Solons and Cassars, except in the British Museum and Chantrey's contracts. A genuine Spaniard would sooner par with his skin than his *capa*; so when Charles III. wanted to prohibit their use, the universal people rose in arms, and the Squillacci, or anti-cloak ministry, was turned out. The *capa* fits its

wearer admirably; it favours habits of inactivity, prevents the over-zealous arms or elbows from doing anything, conceals a knife and rags, and, when muffled around, offers a disguise for intrigues and robbery; *capa y espada* accordingly became the generic term for the profligate comedy which portrayed the age of Philip IV.

[201] Uncloaking is equivalent to taking off the hat; Spaniards always uncloak when *Su Majestad*, the host or the king, passes by; the lower orders uncloak when speaking to a superior: *whenever the traveller sees one not do that with him, let him be on his guard.*

[201] The cloth, from the brown colour, is called "*paño pardo*" and is still the precise mixed red rusty tint for which Spain was renowned...

[202] The *paño pardo* is very thick, not only to last longer, but because the cloak is the shield and buckler of quarrelsome people, who wrap it round the left arm. The assassins of Caesar did the same, when they rushed with their bloody daggers through frightened Rome (App. ' B. C ii. 818). The Spaniards in the streets, the moment the sharp click of the opened knife is heard, or their adversary stoops to pick up a stone, whisk their cloaks round their left arms with marvellous and most classical rapidity.

[276 Seville] The sunny flats under the old Moorish walls, which extend between the gates of *Carmona* and *La Came*, are the haunts of idlers and gamesters. The lower classes of Spaniards are constantly gambling at cards: groups are to be seen playing all day long for wine, love, or coppers, in the sun, or under their vine- trellises. There is generally some well-known cock of the walk, a bully, or *guapo*, who will come up and lay his hand on the cards, and say, "No one shall play here but with mine"— *aqui no se juega sino con mis barajas.* If the gamblers are cowed, they give him *dos cuartos*, a halfpenny each. If, however, one of the challenged be a spirited fellow, he defies him. *Aqui no se cobra el barato sino con tin puñal de Albacete* — "You get no change here except out of an Albacete knife." If the defiance be accepted, *vamos alla* is the answer

—" Let's go to it." There's an end then of the cards, all flock to the more interesting *écarté*; instances have occurred, where Greek meets Greek, of their tying the two advanced feet together, and yet remaining fencing with knife and cloak for a quarter of an hour before the blow be dealt. The knife is held firmly, the thumb is pressed straight on the blade, and calculated either for the cut or thrust, to chip bread and kill men.

The term *Barato* strictly means the present which is given to waiters who bring a new pack of cards. The origin is Arabic, *Baara*, "a *voluntary* gift;" in the corruption of the *Baratero*, it has become an involuntary one: now the term resembles the Greek /βαραθρος, homo perditus, whence the Roman *Balatrones*, the miners of markets, *Barathrumque Macelli*; our legal term *Barratry* is derived from the medieval *Barrateria*, which Ducange very properly interprets as "cheating, foul play." Sancho's sham government was of *Barateria*; *Baratar*, in old Spanish, [277] meant to exchange unfairly, to thimble-rig, to sell anything under its real value, whence the epithet *barato*, cheap. *Baratero* is quite a thing of Spain, where personal prowess is cherished. There is a *Baratero* in every regiment, ship, prison, and even among galleyslaves. For the Spanish knife, its use and abuse, see Albacete.

[407] Guadix is renowned for its knife. *El Cuchillo de Guadix* is made with a *molde*, or catch by which the blade can be fixed and converted into a dagger; admirable for stabbing, nothing can be ruder than this cutlery, which however answers Spanish purposes, and that *guerra al cuchillo*, which proved scarcely less fatal to the invader than the British bayonet (but see Albacete for Spanish knives).

[430 Valencia] Accordingly, in this irritable climate, where the knife is always ready, precautions have long been taken to keep the peace.

Richard Ford (1845, New York) *A Handbook for Travellers in Spain* Volume 2

[719 The Castiles] The *Castellano* is less addicted to murder and treachery than the irritable native of the south and south-east provinces; he may, indeed, be a less agreeable companion than the Ionian *Andaluz*, or plausible *Valenciano*, but like the Spartan, he is a nobler and more male and trustworthy character; he and his provinces are still Robur Hispanise (Flor. ii. 17. 9), and contain the virility, vitality, and heart of the nation, and the sound stuff of which it has to be reconstructed. Meanwhile, the Castilian is not addicted to low degrading vices; although proud, obstinate, ignorant, prejudiced, superstitious, and uncommercial, he is true to his God and king, his religion running often into bigotry, his loyalty into subserviency. These two pivots, these characteristic feelings, still exist, scotched not killed, and the current flows deeply, although silently, under the babble and bubble of recent exotic and most un-Spanish reforms.

Loyal, in the strict meaning of the term *legalis*, he is not, for the law of cities is not the peasant's friend. Their *Justicia*, the very sound of which, like our Chancery, affects every Spaniard high or low with delirium tremens, practically means a denial of justice, and ruin ; it only interferes to punish or oppress; an engine of the strong and rich against weakness and poverty, it never in Spain has been the people's protector; yet, like many *Cosas de España*, the law itself in theory and on paper is good, and requires little change, the one thing wanting is that it should he *fairly administered by upright, honest judges*, which scarcely can be said to exist throughout the Peninsula.

Therefore the Castilian and Spaniard take the law in their own hands, or rather make a new one which is antagonistic and corrective of that framed by their misrulers; and they respect their own *private* code quite as much as they disregard the public one, especially in all *personal* offences; hence the wild justice of their revenge (see p. 145). The bulk of the people sympathise with those who break the public law, especially in cases of smuggling; nevertheless, when not tempted by its all-corrupting profits, the Castillians are moral and well-disposed, and satisfied to leave

things as they are; for they have long enjoyed in practice many republican institutions under a nominal despotism; thus they elect their own *alcaldes* and officers, who in local Spain are the real rulers, both *de jure et facto*; safe in their obscurity, they were indemnified by a liberty of action, which was denied to possessors of rank, wealth, and intellect, who being feared by the king and priest, were accordingly kept down; and this accounts for the apparent anomaly of the lower classes having opposed those reforms which the higher ones coveted; not that the grandees had any much clearer ideas of real constitutional liberty than a debating club of shop-boys. Meanwhile the people, anxious indeed to see the *derechos de puerta* abolished, and tobacco cheaper and better, cared little for theoretical evils, which were neutralized in practice; and as the lower classes are by far the best and finest of Spaniards, so are they the happiest; to them equality, liberty, and safety are realities. They indeed may sing on the high roads, who trust for defence to their own good knife. In this land of contradictions the wealthy have few enjoyments from their wealth, and the poor few denials from their poverty (see pp. 278, 433). The rich must depend on institutions for safety, which here too often injure and seldom protect. No wonder, therefore, that these peasants, as Addison said of those in the Georgics, toss about even manure with an air of dignity; this is the result also of natural instinct even more than of social conventions, since each esteeming himself inferior to none but the king, cares little for the accidents of rank and fortune. Nor does poverty, the great crime never to be pardoned in England, unless it be very grinding, here unfit a person for [720] society, *Pohreza no es vileza*: nor does it destroy personal respectability and independence; indeed, where the majority are poor, the not being rich does not degrade, and an innate gentility of race, which nothing can take away, renders them indifferent to the changes and chances of fickle prosperity, and proud even in rags. The Castellano, an old, although decayed gentleman, never forgets, or permits others to forget, what is due to himself; courteous to others, he expects a reciprocity as regards himself, and when once that is conceded, knows well how to give place. As the beggars cover under the stately *capa* their shreds and patches, so he conceals under an outward lofty bearing his inner feelings; he hopes,

and his motive is honourable, to divert observation by showing a more swelling port than the family means would grant continuance; hence the struggle between ostentation and want, the *Boato* of the *Bisoño*; but "to boast of the national strength is the national disease." See pp. 172, 203, on this head, and the Oriental resignation with which privations are honourably endured.

[723] The average of death at Madrid is as 1 in 28, while in London it is as 1 in 42: no wonder, according to Salas, that even the healthy live on physic.

> "*Aun las personas mas sanas,*   ["Even the healthiest people,
> *Si son en Madrid nacidas,*   If they are born in Madrid,
> *Tienen que hacer sus comidas,*   They have to make their meals,
> *De pildolas y tisanas."*   of pills and herbal tea."]

It is particularly fatal to young children, who during dentition *die como chinches*. The summer scirocco blights vegetation, and by exciting a knife-handling population, fills hospitals with wounded and prisons with murderers.

[733] Observe the singular groups of sallow, unshorn, hungry, bandit-looking men, with fierce-flashing eyes and thread-bare shorn *capas*, which cluster like bees round the reader of some " authentic letter." These form two of the three classes into which a large portion of all who wear long-tailed coats may be divided: first the *Pretendiente*, or place-hunter, who aspires to some situation, a sinecure if possible, his food is hope; next the *Empleado*, or fortunate youth, who has got into a good birth, whose bliss is the certainty of taking bribes, and the chance of being paid the salary of his appointment; and lastly, the *Cesante*, or one who, having held some offices, is now turned out, his joys and profits have ceased, his misery is memory, his consolation revenge. The *Pretendientes y Cesantes* either wear away the thresholds of the minister of the hour, or polish the pavement of the *Puerta del Sol*, with the restlessness of caged wild beasts, for this is the den of the *Empleomanicos*, the victims of that madness for place which is the peculiar disease of Madrid. Hence this their

rendezvous is the mint of scandal, and all who have lived intimately with them know how invariably every one abuses his neighbour behind his back, the lower orders occasionally using a knife, which is sharper even than the tongue. Self, in fact, is every where the idol, for no Spaniard can tolerate a rival or superior.

[738] The dazzling glare and fierce African sun calcining the heavens and earth, fires up man and beast to madness; now in a raging thirst for blood, seen in flashing eyes and the irritable ready knife, how the passion of the Arab triumphs over the coldness of the Goth: how different is the crowd and noisy hurry from the ordinary still life and monotony of these localities. The horrid excitement fascinates the many, like the tragedy of an execution, for, as a lively Frenchman observes, "La réalité atroce is the recreation of the savage, and the sub [739] lime of common-place souls." The quadrupeds are as mad as the bipeds, the poor horses excepted, who are worse baited than the bulls.

[774] Some remarks (see p. 173) have been made on the condition of Spanish hospitals and medical men. They are much deficient, with few exceptions, in all improved mechanical appliances, comforts, and modern discoveries, as is admitted and deplored by all sensible Spaniards. The sanative science does not progress in proportion to the destructive, for the *puñales* of Albacete are better made and more effective than the scalpels; but at no period were Spaniards careful even of their own lives, and much less of those of others, being a people of untender bowels. Familiarity with pain deadens the finer feelings of those employed even in our hospitals, for those who live by the dead have only an undertaker's sympathy for the living, and are as dull to the poetry of innocent health as Mr. Giblet is to a sportive house-fed lamb. Matters are not improved in Spain, where the wounds, blood, and death of the pastime bull-fight, the *muera mobcries*, and *pasarle por las armas*, Draco and Durango decrees, and practices of all in power, educate all sexes to indifference to blood, and the fatal knife-stab or surgeon's cut, as *Cosas de España* and things of course.

[858] Albacete is called the Sheffield of Spain, as Chatelherault is in France; but every thing is by comparison, and the coarse cutlery in each, at whose make and material an English artisan sneers, perfectly answers native ideas and wants. The object of a Spanish knife is to " chip bread and kill a man," and our readers are advised to have as little to do with them as may be. The *cuchillo*, like the fan of the high-bred Andaluza, is part and parcel of all Spaniards of the lower class, who never are without the weapon of offence and defence, which is fashioned like a woman's tongue, being long, sharp, and pointed. The test of a bad knife is, that it won't cut a stick, but will cut a finger, *Cuchillo malo, corta al dado y no alpalo.* This knife, the precise *daga* of the Iberians (for details see Toledo, p. 853), is the national weapon: hence *Guerra al Cuchillo* is the modern warcry which has supplanted the old *algarada of Santiago y Cierra Espana!*

Now Castile expects that every knife this day will do its duty, and such was the truly Spanish war defiance which Palafox at Zaragoza returned to the French summons to capitulate. This " long double-edged " tool is either stuck, as the old dagger used to be, in the sash, or worn in the breeches' side-pocket, where our carpenters carry their rule, like the Greek heroes did their παραμηρια. Such, however, was the Oriental fashion, down the "right thigh" (Judges iii. 16); and so the anelace in Chaucer bare "a Shefeild thwitel in his hose," just as the *Manolas,* or Amazons of Madrid, conceal a small knife in their garters by way of "steel traps set here." This trinket is also called a *puñaleco* and *higuela,* which, strictly speaking, means a "petticoat bustle;" and all these weapons are akin to the Mattucashlash dirk, which the Scotch Highlanders carried in their arm-pits: a feminine *puñaleco* now before us has the motto, *Sirbo á una Dama,* I serve a lady — Ich Dien. Gentlemen's knives have also what Shakspere calls their "cutler poetry," and it is a Moorish custom, for [859] our friend Gayangos has traced in what appeared to be a mere scrolly ornament, on a modern Albacete *cuchillo,* these Arabic words, " With the help of Allah! I hope to kill my enemy."

Thus the Spanish manufacturers have many centuries worked after the same pattern, and for the same beneficent object, each operative copying his model by a certain instinct, without even understanding the meaning

of what he is rudely scratching on the blade. The mottos of the Toledan rapiers were superb (see p. 854). and those on the knives follow at a humbler pace; e. g., *Soy de mi Dueno y Señor*, "I am the thing of my lord and master." So Nero's poignard was inscribed "*Jovi Vindici*" (Tac. 'An.' xv. 74). When the *Sistema*, or *constitution* of 1820, was put down, royalist knives were inscribed *Peleo á gusto matando negros*, and on the reverse, *Muero por mi Rey*, "I die for my king; killing blacks is my delight." The words *Negros* and *Carboneros* have long been applied in Spain to political *black*guards, who are whipped and hung with as little scruple in benighted despotised Spain as niggars are in free and enlightened America.

The term *Navaja* means any blade which shuts into a handle, from a razor to a penknife: the *Navajas* of Guadix, which rival the *Puñales* of Albacete, have frequently a *molde muelle* or catch, by which the long pointed blade is fixed, and thus becomes a dagger or hand bayonet. The click which the cold steel makes when sharply caught in its catch, produces on Spanish ears the same pleasing sensation which the cocking a pistol does on ours. The gipsies being great hole-in-corner men and cutpurses, *Rinconetes y Cortadillos*, and patrons of slang and flash men, have furnished many cant names to knife, e. g. *glandi, chulo, churri, La Serdanie, Cachas dos puñales a una vez*; the Catalans call it *El gavinete*. It is termed in playful metaphor *La tia*, my aunt; *Corta pluma*, a penknife; *Monda dientes*, a tooth-pick; and the Spaniards are quite as learned in its make and cut. Thus Sancho Panza, when he hears that Montesinos had pierced a heart with a *puñal*, exclaims at once, "Then it was made by Ramon Hozes of Seville."

However unskilled the regular *Sangrados* may be in anatomy and use of the scalpel, the universal people know exactly how to use their knife, and where to plant its blow; nor is there any mistake, for the wound, although not so deep as a well, nor so wide as a church door, " 'twill serve." It is uusally [print error] given after the treacherous fashion of their Oriental and Iberian ancestors, and if possible by a stab behind, of which the ancients were so fearful, "*impacatos a tergo horrebis Iberos*" (Geor. iii. 408), and "under the fifth rib," and "one blow " is enough (2 Sam. xx. 10). The blade, like the cognate Arkansas or Bowie knife of the

Yankees, will "rip up a man right away," or drill him until a surgeon can see through his body. As practice makes perfect, a true *Baratero* is able to jerk his *navaja* into a door the room, as surely and quickly a rifle ball; a Spaniard, when armed with his *cuchillo* for attack, and with his *capa* for defence, is truly formidable and classical (see p. 202, 276). Many of the murders in Spain must be attributed to the readiness of the weapon, which is always at hand when the blood is on fire: thus where an unarmed Englishman closes his fist, a Spaniard opens his knife. This rascally instrument, a true *puñalada de picaro*, becomes fatal in jealous broils, when the lower classes light their anger at the torch of the furies, and prefer using to speaking daggers: then the thrust goes home, *vitamque in vulnere ponit*. The numbers killed on great festivals exceeds those of most Spanish battles in the field, yet the occurrence is scarcely noticed in the newspapers, so much is it a matter of course; but crimes which call forth a second edition and double sheet in our papers, are slurred over on the continent, for foreigners conceal what we most display.

In minor cases of flirtation, where [860] capital punishment is not called for, the offended party just gashes the cheek of the peccant one, and suiting the word to the action observes, "*ya estas senalaā;* " Now you are marked again, "*Mira que te pego. Mira que te mato*" are playful fondling expressions of a *Maja* to a *Majo*. When this particular mark is only threatened, the Seville phrase was "*Mira que te pinto un jabeque*" take care that I don't draw you a xebeck (the sharp Mediterranean felucca). "They jest at wounds who never felt a scar," but whenever this *jabeque* has really been inflicted, the patient, ashamed of the stigma, is naturally anxious to recover a good character and skin, which only one cosmetic can effect; this in Philip IV/s time was cat's grease, which then removed such superfluous marks,

  El selo unto de gato,   [The ointment of the cat,
  Que en cara dejienda los senales. Heal scars on the face]

Emile Andre (1910) *L'art de se defendre dans la Rue*
(Art of Defence in the Street)

(translated from original French)
(1) There are other kinds of guards advised by Spanish fencers. (We know that in Spain, the navaja, a kind of large knife, and ordinary knives are practiced more than in other countries.)

With the navaja, one guard consists of standing forward, both feet on the same line and alternately passing the weapon from one hand to the other. But it is specified that these changes of hand (*cambios*), which must be done very quickly, require a lot of practice.

Let's say for now, without going back, that, in the books published in Spain on fencing with the knife, one reads without doubt excellent advice and ingenious tricks, but there is not enough recognition of the role already indicated that the strikes of French and English boxing can play, even in knife combat.

(1) Certain turning movements are used in the Spanish play of which we have spoken in a previous note. A twisting motion, or jiro, is performed, a "turn" that the opponent avoids by turning on their side, performing a contra-jiro a "counter-turn". (Sometimes, in response, we use this contra-jiro to attack the opponent at the same time, making a new jiro opposite to the first. Hand changes are sometimes combined, using the navaja, with these movements.)

These various turns require a lot of practice and are still very risky.

Theophile Gautier (1901) *Travels in Spain*

At Santa Cruz we were asked to purchase all sorts of pocket knives -- *navajas*. Santa Cruz and Albacete are famous for fancy cutlery. The *navajas*, made in the most characteristic Arabic and barbaric taste, have open-worked handles through which show red, green, or blue spangles. Coarse inlaid work, but designed with dash, adorns the blade, which is fish-shaped and always very sharp. Most of them have mottoes, such as Soy de uno solo (I am one man's), or Cuando esta vivora pica, no hay remedio en la botica (When this adder stings, there is no antidote in the pharmacy). Sometimes the blade is rayed with three parallel lines inlaid in red, which gives it a most formidable appearance. The size of the *navaja* varies from three inches to three feet in length. Some majos (peasants of the better class) carry some which, when opened, are as long as a sabre. A spring or a ring to which a turn is given secures the blade in a straight line. The *navaja* is the favourite weapon of the Spaniards, especially of the country people. They use it with incredible dexterity, wrapping their cloak around their arm by way of buckler. The science of the *navaja* has its professors like fencing, and *navaja*-teachers are as numerous in Andalusia as fencing-masters in Paris. Each *navaja* expert has his secret lunges and his own particular strokes. It is said that adepts can tell by looking at a wound to what artist it is due, just as we can tell a painter by the touch of his brush.

I'm intrigued by the claim that "adepts can tell by looking at a wound to what artist it is due," implying that every knife-wielder inflicts enough wounds on different victims that a recognizable pattern is established. That reminds me of the scene in The Good, the Bad, and the Ugly in which Clint Eastwood recognizes his opponent from the sound of distant gunfire, observing, "Every gun makes its own tune."

Henry George O'Shea (1889) *O'Shea's Guide to Spain and Portugal*

La *navaja*, or *cuchillo*, often as long as a common sword, settles at once all differences of opinion, blood being thought to wipe off any petty rancour. It is used very frequently, and has become an art in which the *barateros* are proficient. A *baratero* (from *barato*, cheap) lives by his knife. He frequents gambling circles, and receives some coins from the cowed-down players whom he has threatened to disturb if they should not grant his boon. This is called *cobrar el barato*, "to get change." In some cases, one of the challenged parties gets up and refuses to pay; upon which the champion fights. Death often ensues, as the stomach is aimed at. Those curious to learn more particulars may consult '*Manual del Baratero*,' with prints. The best specimens of knives can be had at Madrid and Seville; they are principally manufactured at Albacete; they have bright colours on the blade, with mottoes; a muelle or catch; the price varies from 6r. to 30r.

Samuel Parsons Scott (1886) *Through Spain: a Narrative of Travel and Adventure in the Peninsula*

The *baratero* is a character not peculiar to Malaga, but who attains his highest development in that city. The word means, in plain language, a blackmailer of gamblers. This ruffian rarely plays himself, but never fails to be on hand when a game is in progress. After the winner has gathered in the stakes, he pays over a certain proportion—usually five per cent—of the profits to the *baratero*. If any hesitation is manifested to submit to this extortion, a fight is inevitable, and, as the *baratero* is always an adept in the use of the knife, he is morally certain to get the better of his opponent, who loses at the same time his money and his life. No amount is too trifling for the consideration of this ravenous bird of prey, who pockets a few cuartos with the haughty insolence with which he demands a doubloon. The quarters of the city frequented by gamblers are divided into districts by the *barateros*, each of whom, inspired by that traditional sentiment of honor common to criminals, is careful not to encroach upon

the province of any of his brethren; the danger of such interference, moreover, being aptly expressed by the saying, "*Nadie se meta a Baratero sin contar antes con los Eserilanos.*" ("Settle with the magistrates before picking a quarrel with a *baratero*.")

The skill displayed by the Spanish desperado in handling his knife is wonderful. This weapon, to which all are so partial, is a wicked-looking affair, from one to two feet long, and called a *navaja* from its resemblance to a razor. The blade is of the finest Toledo steel, and bears the motto common to the side-arms forged upon the famous Tagus: "No me saques sin razon; No me envainen sin honor." ("Do not draw me without cause; Do not sheathe me without honor.")

Defence with the *navaja* has been reduced to a science, which has its regular school of instruction. The teachers give lessons with wooden knives, and the most noted among them have their private strokes, which are kept secret for cases of emergency. The arts of the most accomplished swordsman are worthless, when opposed to those of an expert with the *navaja*. With his cloak or jacket wrapped about his left arm, his formidable weapon glittering in his right hand, and his lithe body poised for a spring, he is an interesting study for the spectator, as well as for his antagonist. The thumb is pressed tightly along the back of the blade, that every advantage may be taken of the flexibility of the wrist, in a struggle where the space of an inch is often a matter of life and death. The postures and guards are changed with bewildering rapidity, and, should the right hand be disabled, the cloak and knife are shifted in the twinkling of an eye, and the duel proceeds, until one or both the combatants are killed.

Hand-to-hand encounters are most esteemed by professors of the *navaja*, but there is a class of them who make a specialty of lodging the weapon from a distance in the vitals of an enemy. They become perfect by throwing it at a peseta fastened to a piece of cork, the coin becoming the prize of the winner. When one grows skillful enough to hit the mark twice in three times, at ten paces, he is ruled out of the contest, and is recognized as a diestro. The blades of these knives are contrived with

devilish ingenuity so as to inflict painful and incurable wounds, and are grooved, like Indian arrows, to permit the blood to run freely. All the thrusts and parries used by experts have their technical names—the *navaja* itself being termed an abanico (" fan")— which are as unintelligible to the non-professional as those belonging to the comprehensive jargon of the bull-fighter.

Edmondo De Amicis (1880) *Spain and the Spaniards*

In passing through a solitary little street, I saw in the show-window of a hardware establishment a collection of such immensely long, broad knives that I was instantly seized by the desire to purchase one. I entered; twenty or more were spread out for my inspection, and I had them opened one by one. Every time a blade was opened I gave a step backward. [Me: Wouldn't he soon have stepped out of the shop?] I do not believe one can imagine a more horrible or barbarous-looking weapon than this, which has a copper, brass, or horn handle, is slightly curved, and cut in open work which shows little streaks of various-colored isinglass, opens with a noise like that of a rattle, and out comes a blade as broad as your hand, and two palms in length, in the shape of a fish, as sharp as a dagger, and ornamented with chasings colored red (so that they look like stains of congealed blood), and menacing and ferocious inscriptions. On one is written in Spanish: "Do not open me without cause, or close me without honor"; on another: "Where I touch all is finished"; on a third: "When this snake bites no physician is of any avail; " and other pleasant mottoes of the same nature.

The proper name of these knives is *navaja,* which also means razor, and the *navaja* is the weapon with which the common people fight their duels. Now, it has rather fallen into disuse, but once it was in great demand. There were masters in this art, each one of whom had his secret thrust, and the people fought duels in accordance with all the rules of the cavaliers. I purchased the most enormous *navaja* in the shop, and we continued our route.

Look at the size of this thing! It's so impractical--so why do I want one? On reaching Castillejo I was obliged to wait until midnight for the train for Andalusia . . . when I got into a railway carriage filled with women, boys, civil guards, cushions, and wraps; and away we went at a speed unusual on Spanish railways. . . . I fell asleep after a few moments. I think I had already dreamed of the Mosque of Cordova and the Alcazar of Seville, when I was awakened by a hoarse cry: "Daggers!"

"Daggers? In heaven's name! For whom?"
Before I saw who had shouted, a long sharp blade gleamed before my eyes, and the unknown person asked: "Do you like it?"

One must really confess that there are more agreeable ways of being waked. I looked at my travelling companions with an expression of stupor which made them all burst out into a hearty laugh. Then I was told that at every railway station there were these venders of knives and daggers, who offered travellers their wares just as newspapers and refreshments are offered with us. Reassured as to my life, I bought (for five lire) my scarecrow, which was a beautiful dagger suitable for the tyrant of a tragedy, with its chased handle, an inscription on the blade, and an embroidered velvet sheath; and I put it in my pocket, thinking that it would be quite useful to me in Italy in settling any questions with my publishers.

The vender must have had fifty of them in a great red sash which was fastened around his waist. Other travellers bought them too; the civil guards complimented one of my neighbors on his capital selection; the boys cried: "Give me one too!" - and their mammas replied: "We will buy a longer one some other time."

"O blessed Spain!" I exclaimed, as I thought, with disgust, of our barbarous laws which prohibit the innocent amusement of a little sharp steel.

GLOSSARY:

Alfileres: Pin. Slang for knife.

Armas blancas: white weapon. Sharp / real weapons.

Armas negra: Black weapon. Practice weapons, blunt, with a covered or blunted point.

Arrieros: Muleteer, mule driver. A person who manages horses and mules for travel and transport of goods between towns. Connected to the word *ordinarios*.

Attracar: To get stuck. Slang for a stab.

Baratero: One who deals, or barters.

Barato: Cheap. From many Romance languages; Spanish, Portuguese, Galician, Latino. In Spanish / Andalusian it is often used as slang to refer to the money that thugs take from gamblers or the less fortunate.

Baratar: To barter. An outdated verb.

Barrio: District.

Caballeros: Horseman, gentlemen, knight (title implying courtesy and respect)

Casa de poco trigo: Prison. The 'house of little wheat' (the house of the scarce money). Also *estarivél*.

Cachas: Scissors or shears (Calo), See *tijeras*.

Calabozero: Prison guards.

Camino: Path or way.

Canalla: Riffraff, rabble, swine, those of the gutter. Used by upper class to describe the lower class.

Cambios: Changes. Referring to changing the *navaja* or knife from one hand to another.

Cantinas: A mess hall or servery. Also taverns and bars.

Cantinera: Barmaid, serving girl.

Charranes: Tern (like a seagull). Slang for rascals and villains, also fish sellers on the street.

Chebek: See *jabeque*

Chirlo: Slash or scar upon the face. See *jabeque*.

Cobraor: One who charges the commission in gambling ie the *baratero*

Cobro / Cobrar: To charge or swindle a portion of money in gambling, often with violence, or threat of.

Contrajiro: A counter turn. The counter to the *jiros*. Moving backwards in a mirrored response to the turning footwork of the *jiro*.

Contrario: The opponent. The adversary in a fight; opposed to the *diestro*.

Corridas: A run. Closely associated with an action performed in bullfighting. Circling of an opponent to find or force an opening.

Cortaplumas: Pocket knife or pen knife.

Cuchillo: A fixed bladed knife, not folding like the *navaja*.

Culebra: Snake.

Desjarretazo(s): To thrust down with reverse grip behind shoulder blade and slice outwards. Related to the word jarret; to hamstring. Closely associated with the *Coup de Jarnac*.

Destreza: Skill. Specifically regards fighting with sword or knife.

Diestro: Right handed, or skilled. Used to refer to a skilled person, a user of knife or sword. In the context of the Manual it refers to the user of the *navaja*, and the opponent is the *contrario*.

Ejecutan: Execute, to carry out, to do.

Estarivél: Jail. Also known as *casa de poco trigo*.

Enfilar: Wounding the face. A deeply insulting strike. See *jabeque*.

Engaños: Deceits, deceptions, Dee *recursos*.

Esquiladores: Farriers and shearers of donkeys, horses, and mules, most often *jitanos*.

Faja: Sash belt

Finjimientos: Feints, pretenses. See *recursos*.

Floretazos: A counter cut, most often in the *parte alta* (upper part). The word *floret* is used to mean the foil (blunted weapon to represent the sword or sabre), and *tazar* is to cut, thus the *floretazos* is a cut performed with a foil, or against the weapon arm. Usually considered quick and agile.

Garitos: Gambling den.

Gitanos: See *jitanos*.

Golpes: Blows. Referring to all manner of cuts and thrusts. Relevant to the weapon being used.

Golpes de costado: Blows to the flank or side.

Herramienta: Tool. Slang name for knife. See *navaja*.

Hierros: Iron. Slang name for knife. See *navaja*.

Huide / Huida: Also *huye*. Escape / void. A movement of the body to avoid incoming incoming attacks. Closely related to *quites / quitar*.

Huye: Escape / flee.

Jabeque / Javeque: *Chebek, xebec, zebec.* A Mediterranean three-masted sailing ship, used mostly for trading. A small, fast vessel of the sixteenth to nineteenth centuries, used almost exclusively in the Mediterranean Sea. The slang name for a cut to the face, reminiscent of the diagonal angle of the sails.

Jiro(s): Turn. A circling step.

Jitanos: Spanish word used to describe gypsies, or Romani people. Also used to describe rural people. Commonly used in a derogatory manner.

Lazzarone: Italian slang; a person dominated by shrewd greed or an indisposing laziness. However it can also imply an intimate and resentful hostility, alluding to the ability to commit seriously reprehensible actions.

Los hombres del pueblo: Men of the town, referring to common people.

Manera: The manner.

Manolas: Woman of the people, characterised by flamboyant zarzuela-type costume.

Manta: Mantle or cape.

Matones: Bullies, thugs.

Medios: The means. The measures, way of, or the method of which to undertake *modo, manera, suerte*.

Modo: The way, the method. Related in usage to (from most detailed to least): *modo, manera, suerte*, and *medios*.

Mojo: A stab. See *attracar, puñala, viaje*.

Mondadientes: Toothpick. Slang for knife. See *navaja*.

Molinete: Wheel. A spinning defensive response, and sometimes counter attack.

Navaja: A folding knife. Later with a locking mechanism. Most often associated with a specific blade shape and ratcheting 'click click click' sound. There are numerous slang names for various knives: *abanico* (fan), alfiler (pin), the *chaira* (steel), *cortaplumas* (pocketknife), *corte* (sharp), *cuchillo* (knife), *herramienta* (tool), *hierro* (iron), *mojosa* (the moistened / bloodied), *mondadientes* (toothpick), *pincho* (skewer), *puñal* (stilletto), the *tea* (a small spike; the tool used to break up tea cake tea leaves that have been compressed for storage and transport).

Ordinarios: Ordinary. Also used as a catch all word for common, coarse or rude people, the rabble.

Parte alta: The high part (target area) – the body above the waist sash.

Parte baja: The low part (target area) – the body below the waist sash.

Presidios: Garrisons. Used for both jails and military fortifications. Spain often used prisoners to build such fortresses such as *Seuta* (*Ceuta*).

Pueblo: Town or village. Also used to refer to 'the people'.

Plumada: Feather or flourish. The blow or stab struck from right to left, generally describing a curve.

Puñal: A stabbing style knife, like a stiletto.

Puñala/da: Stabbing attack.

Quite / Quitar: Retreat / remove. A movement out of the way, usually including a redirection of the incoming attack, sometimes using a quarter *plumada* strike to counter cut the attacking hand. Closely related to *huida*.

Recortes: To cut away, to cut out or to cut off. A dangerous voiding movement forward into an attack, turning the back to an opponent. The opposite of a *contrajiros* (in moving forwards rather than backwards). This action is seen in acrobatic demonstrations against a charging bull.

Recursos: Recourses. Similar in meaning to responses, resources, or options. The action taken when the basic destreza skills are not enough to win. These actions include *engaños* or *finjimientos*, and *tretas*.

Reves: Backhand or reverse. The blow struck with the hand turned outwards and from left to right.

Serenos: (of Malaga) Night watchmen and key custodians.

Sombrero de teja: Tile hat, worn by Catholic clergymen.

Suerte: True translation is fortune (luck, fate or chance). It can also be a kind, sort, class or manner (as in type of object). Usage: *de suerte que*; in such a manner. It is a somewhat contextual word referring to the type of thing that is being discussed. For the translation generally I have used 'technique' as this best fits English usage, unless context is obviously otherwise.

Tahúres: Card sharps, gamblers, cheats, craven.

Terreno: The terrain. Referring to the ground within reach of the *diestro*, the space between the fighters.

Tijeras: Scissors or shears, *caches*. The *jitanos* were known to maintain horses and other livestock, and involved in the making of playing (and tarot) cards, closely connected to gambling and the *baratero*.

Tiradore(s): Term given to one who fights with a knife. Modern usage is marksman or sharpshooter. Similar in construction to *matador* (bullfighter), *tire* is to shoot, or to cut.

Trabuco: Catapult. Slang for blunderbuss or pistol. Also slang for prick and a name for a knife.

Trajinero: Boat rower. The *trajinero* is a boat still seen in Mexico, pushed along the canals with poles, similar to Venetian Gondolieri, to move people and freight.

Tretas: Tricks. Secret strikes. See *recursos*.

Viaje(s): Trip or voyage.

NOTES:

1. Few works by common and *verdadera destreza* authors are available in English, but there are some. For Further reading about common fencing see *Common Iberian Fencing*, translated by Tim Rivera (2016) originally written by Domingo Luis Godinho (1599). For further reading about *la verdadera destreza*, visit www.destreza.us, which hosts partial translations of Francisco Antonio de Ettenhard's *Compendium of the Foundations of the True Art and Philosophy of Arms*, translated by Dr Mary Curtis. Gérard Thibault d'Anvers' work, *Academy of the Sword*, is also arguably part of the *destreza* tradition. Two translations are available in bookstores today.
2. *Cocinero, cocinera*: these in modern language are simply masculine and feminine versions of the word 'cook', however in the 19th century, *cocinero* would have been a professional cook or chef, and *cocinera* would be kitchenmaids. *Botillero* has no direct cultural or literal translation. Essentially a *botillería* was a place where people could gather and drink refreshing beverages that weren't tea or coffee and could also buy ice cream, all of which were made on the premises by the *botillero*. Therefore, the term has been left untranslated.
3. We know this detail from an obituary published by Rementaria's friend and collaborator, Antonio de Iza Zamacola, in a periodical Revista de Teatros. From Ucelay da Cal, Margarita (1951). Los españoles pintados por sí mismos (1843-1844) Estudio de un género costumbrista. México: El Colegio de México, pg. 45.
4. During the Peninsular Wars and following French occupation of Spain martial law was introduced, making it an executable offence to carry any kind of weapon, including scissors and knives. The quote refers to the uprising of Dos de Mayo, the 2nd of May. https://en.wikipedia.org/wiki/Dos_de_Mayo_Uprising. Quoted is Maximilien Sébastien Foy (3 February 1775 – 28 November 1825) a French military leader, statesman and writer including a history of the Peninsular War. https://en.wikipedia.org/wiki/Maximilien_Sebastien_Foy
5. Ohnimus, Luis Juan (1890) 'Six inches of steel: Bowie knife fighting instruction', *St Louis Republic*, 14 June. Transcription available at http://www.stickgrappler.net/2013/05/six-inches-of-steel-bowie-knife.html And other such newspaper articles in 19th century USA.
6. *L'art de se defendre dans la rue* (French), Emile Andre, 1910

7. *Demófilo* (Antonio Machado y Álvarez) wrote two seminal collections: *Colección de cantes flamencos*, Seville, 1881 and *Cantes flamencos y cantares*, Madrid, 1887.
8. *Cantes Flamencos*, Michael Smith & Luis Ingelmo, 2012. This book also gives some tantalising connections between the art of the Navaja and the arts of flamenco and tango, hinted at in discussions with Oscar Reyes.

THE TRANSLATION: PROLOGUE

9. During the 15th to 19th C in Spain were numerous royal 'decrees' which were listings of laws and legislation.
10. A *cátedra* is a cathedral, literally the seat of a bishop in a church. In a Church context, it is a direct reference to the 'authority to teach', granted by the apostles to subsequent bishops in the church. A *cátedra* isn't just a chair, it is specifically a piece of furniture that symbolises this authority. In this passage, the author is mocking those fencing masters, saying that the students that come out of the masters' schools (who come from a questionable teaching authority that's not governed by ACTUAL authorities) are nothing but brutes and murderers. He mocks these fencing masters by comparing their questionable authority to teach with the vaunted 'Divine Authority' the *cátedra* represents for the Church; which in itself is somewhat blasphemous, but that's part of the sting. (Thanks to Lois Spangler)
11. Teresa Castellanos de Mesa y del Castillo was a fencing prodigy. Born in 1817, she inherited her father's passion (Manuel Castellanos de Mesa, Fencing teacher in several institutions, including the corps Guardias de Corps and the Royal Seminary of Nobles of Madrid). When she was very young, she began to make public exhibitions in which she showed her skill before an audience attracted by the unheard of situation: a woman showing the exercise of weapons (in Spain and France). Renowned for her skill with weapons, she opened academies of fencing, calisthenics, and gymnastic in both Spain and France.

THE TRANSLATION: FIRST PART

12. Different blade shapes require the use of different blows. The *navaja* is curved and thus cuts are best used. Originally a folding knife would not be used for thrusts as it did not lock in place, and a thrust risked the blade closing on the users fingers. The *cuchillo* tended to have a straight blade which is not so suited to the slice, and the *puñal* is best for stabbing.
13. Ways of placing the feet.
14. Let the opponent attack first so you can see what he can do.
15. The reference to the *faja* (sash) helping to resist the desjarretazos implies that this technique can be done around the side and waist, not just over the shoulder– refer to references in *MdB* regarding *desjarretazos* and *viaje*.
16. Syrupy mummy's boy or slick–haired dandy. An insult.

THE TRANSLATION: SECOND PART

17. *Vacios* – gaps on the sides; the waist and between the ribs, not just to the sides but also around the back – refer to the *desjarretazos*.
18. Colloquial "to provoke".

THE TRANSLATION: THIRD PART

19. Armguard of woven cane or leather vambrace.
20. *Clava:* to club, *clavar:* to hammer / drive / thrust.
21. The image shows the left hand raised without the hat in hand.
22. This action is essentially an arm-bar throw of the opponent.
23. 'Resolution' is used in Iberian fencing to describe a finishing movement, through disarm or complete control of the opponent. It could refer to the opponent having missed his attack and reseting, or getting up after being thrown.

THE TRANSLATION: FOURTH PART

24. *Pollinos*: ass or donkey also can mean idiots (the *jitanos* were also known as makers of playing cards which used scissors).

THE TRANSLATION: BARATERO

25. Forgive me: a statement made by an executor / hang man before doing his duty.
26. *Canaria del pan*: wind pipe.
27. *Corbatin del vizcaya* – Biscayan Bowtie. Slang for the executioner's garrote, the Spanish form of capital punishment, a particularly brutal way of execution. Introduced in 1813 and used up until 1977. Most commonly the victim sat on a bench against an upright board, with rope around the neck and fed through a hole in the board, tied to a wooden handle which was turned to constrict the noose. https://en.wikipedia.org/wiki/Garrote
28. Calo is the Iberian Romani language, and is related to the word dark, or dark skinned. In the first description there is reference to good looks, then there is reference to being ugly! Apparently one can be cool and ugly at the same time!
29. A fashionable style moustache with points curled upwards.
30. Long nails is a reference to being good at thieving.
31. "*Quitame alla esas pajas*" is a 16th century idiom. It shows up in Don Quixote, translated as "[in] the twinkling of an eye".
32. *Copas ó* cañitas: cups of wine and cups of liqueur.
33. Indicating the ensuing fight was like the Trojan War.
34. The sash was used as a pocket, or place to hide useful items.
35. Shirt sleeves rolled up and bare chested.
36. *Pañuelo de yerbas* (hierbas) a handkerchief or bandana / scarf with a woven cross hatched pattern (like grass).
37. *Arropiero*: maker of syrupy sweet cakes. *Turronero*: maker of sweet nougat.
38. Various card games: *cané* derived from '*sacanete*' itself derived from *lanskenette, lansquenet, landsknecht*, a German Swiss mercenary foot soldier, commonplace in Western Europe during the 16th Century. There is also another common game of cups, where a coin, ball or similar is hidden under moving cups that are moved around and player has to guess where it is. *Pecao* from *peccadillo*: minor sin. In all these ethnic groups is also a card game, played with the traditional "Tarot de Marseilles" deck design, whose surviving variants are still popular.
39. *Cuartos*: quarter, a quarter of a peseta (coin).

40. A style of sideburns which extends along the jaw to the chin (mutton chops). *boca de* jacha: horse mouth, *patillitas de boca e jacha* (mouth jacket sideburns), a comic form of '*patillas de boca ancha*': wide mouth sideburns.
41. *El Perchel* is one of the oldest neighborhoods in *Málaga*. It was built right outside the original city walls and a lot of fishermen and their families lived there. The name of the neighborhood comes from those original fishermen who used to hang the fish to dry. In Spanish, the word "hanger" is "*percha*" and from there, the name "*El Perchel*." It was not always the most desirable place to live, as you can imagine all that drying fish caused quite a smell on a hot day. However nowadays there is a real sense of pride in the neighborhood. It's almost like a badge of honor to say that you are a "*Perchelero*" (someone who is from El Perchel).
https://uncoveringspain.com/spain-guide/malaga-neighborhood-el-perchel/
42. Related to the word *sonsonete*. meaning to tap, or with a sing-song or monotonous delivery, or sarcastic, or mocking undertone. This is threatening action or exclamation of impatience like tapping of the foot.
43. *Ajuma el pescao*: overcooks the fish, to lose your temper.
44. An exclamation.

THE TRANSLATION: POEM

45. The poem describes the different types and traits of *baratero* as does the prose before it. The first verse is about the gambling *baratero*, the second is about the army *baratero*, the third is about he jail *baratero*, the fourth about the smuggler, and the fifth about the womaniser.
46. There is a double meaning here: I kill any who complain, that I get the commission (charge a fee). The *baratero* kills or chases away, even with threat of violence, those who might not fall for his tricks.
47. The *baratero* take his fee and swindles money from the cunning and the clueless alike.
48. I charge. it must be understood that there are significant sinister undertones to this, combining ideas of swindling, trickery, and violence to obtain money.
49. Referring to the various gambling games played in gambling dens, on the streets, on the beach, in the jails, in the soldiers quarters; coins, cards, cups, and just about anything else that can be bet upon. "*en las chapas y el cané*." Street slang (possibly

from the Romani languages (Calo). Las Chapas is a simple street gambling game, based on betting on heads/tails, sometimes played with bottle caps. El cané is gambling card game. Whilst these generally refer to specific games, usage here is reference to any kind of gambling game, played in gambling dens, on the streets, on the beach, in the jails, in the soldiers quarters; coins, cards, cups, and just about anything else that can be bet upon, which the *baratero* may use to swindle money from the unsuspecting.

50. To cough. However this is a complex colloquialism, seen in two other places in the Manual, which refers to making and taking challenges. This line essentially means 'where the *baratero* goes and takes his dues, there are no challengers.' It also refers to being the best at something; 'You cant cough at him' - He's really skilled. from the Real Academia Espanola https://dle.rae.es/toser Competir con ella en algo y especialmente en valor. (To compete with [a person] in something, and especially something valorous or courageous.)
51. 51 *Ternejal*: rogue. Sometimes used in disrespect "all hat, no cowboy", "all talk, no action".
52. *Chichipe* is Calo, Iberian Romani language, thus connecting the poem to Romani culture and implying connection of *baratero* and n*avaja* to the Romani. https://en.m.wikipedia.org/wiki/Caló_language The word is exclamatory meaning 'Awesome!', and refers to how awesome is the *baratero* and his life.
53. *Seuta* is a Spanish city on the coast of North Africa). Prison in Ceuta https://elfarodeceuta.es/el-antiguo-presidio-de-ceuta-en-1850/
54. *Peinao* is an ornamental comb often worn by flamenco dancers.

L'ESPAGNE

55. *Cosas de Espana*: things of Spain. A commonly used phrase at the time to describe culturally and socially unique Spanish ways and traditions.
56. A sheet of thin metallic foil used decoratively in enameling and gilding.
57. Unction. The action of anointing someone with oil or ointment as a religious rite or as a symbol of investiture as a monarch, or treatment with a medicinal oil or ointment.
58. Meaning the authors were not used to the use of sharp weapons.
59. *Coup du Commandeur*. This is another reference to the Coup de Jarnac, a hamstring cut, and the name is closely associated with the *desjarretazos*.
From "Proverbs et dictions de France et leurs equivalents russes" [French proverbs and sayings and their Russian equivalents], 2015, В. Когут. Coup de Jarnac, Coup de commandeur. Is said in talking of a ruse, of a deft or unexpected maneuver through allusion to the duel which took place on 10 July 1547 between Guy de Chabot, Baron Jarnac, and Francois de Vivonne. Jarnac, with a reverse [ed: or "reverse stroke"] of his sword, slices the hamstring [ed: lit. "fendit le jarret"] of his opponent." (Thanks to Chris Slee).
Also: https://www.martinez-destreza.com/products/duel-between-jarnac-and-chateigneraie
60. A prison mentioned in the final poem of the *Manual del Baratero*.
61. *"Ite, missa est"* are the concluding Latin words addressed to the people at the end of Mass "Go, Mass is ended".
62. The Guadalmedina is a river that runs through the city of Málaga, Spain. Historically, it has played an important role in the city's history, and has divided the city into two halves.
63. *Cara y cruz*, face and cross, reference to the gambling game of coin tossing, the same as heads or tails.
64. Reference to those who are of the 'other', the lower class of society. Likely precursor of the word *gringo* originally referred to any kind of foreigner. It was first recorded in 1787 in the Spanish *Diccionario castellano con las voces de Ciencias y Artes:*. GRINGOS, llaman en Málaga a los extranjeros, que tienen cierta especie de acento, que los priva de una locución fácil, y natural Castellana; y en Madrid dan el mismo, y por la misma causa con particularidad a los Irlandeses. *Gringos* is what, in Malaga,

they call foreigners who have a certain type of accent that prevents them from speaking Castilian easily and naturally; and in Madrid they give the same name, and for the same reason, in particular to the Irish. The most likely theory is that it originates from *griego* ('Greek'), used in the same way as the English phrase "it's Greek to me". Spanish is known to have used Greek as a stand-in for incomprehensibility, though now less common, such as in the phrase *hablar en griego* (lit. 'to speak Greek'). The 1817 *Nuevo diccionario francés-español*, for example, gives *gringo* and *griego* as synonyms in this context: ... *hablar en griego, en guirigay, en gringo. Gringo, griego: aplícase a lo que se dice o escribe sin entenderse.* ... to speak in Greek, in gibberish, in gringo.

Gringo, Greek: applied to what is said or written but not understood. From Wikipedia https://en.wikipedia.org/wiki/Gringo

65. This is only a part of the poem at the end of the *Manual del Baratero*.

BIBLIOGRAPHY

Andre, Emile (1910) *L'art de se defendre dans la Rue (Art of Defence in the Street)*

Anonymous (1845, Madrid) *Manual Del Baratero*

Borrow, George. (1841, London) *Zincali: An Account of the gypsies of Spain*

Castle, Egerton (1885, London) *Schools and Masters of Fence from the middle ages to the eighteenth century*

Cherevichnik, Denis. (2018, Riga) *Footnote Manual del Baratero* (Russian), translated by James Wran

Davillier, Baron Charles (1874, Paris) *L'Espagne,* illustrated by Gustav Dore, translated by James Wran

De Amicis, Edmondo (1880) *Spain and the Spaniards,* Translated by Wilhelmina W. Cady

Esdaile, Charles (2003) *The Peninsular War – A New History*

Ford, Richard. (1845, New York) *A Handbook for Travellers in Spain Volume 1 & 2*

Gautier, Théophile (1901) *Travels in Spain*

Hutton, Alfred (1889) *Cold Steel: The Art of Fencing with the Sabre*

Loriega, James (2005) Manual of the Baratero, Paladin Press

Ohnimus, Louis Juan (1890) 'Six inches of steel: Bowie knife fighting instruction', *St Louis Republic,* 14 June. Transcription available at http://www.stickgrappler.net/2013/05/six-inches-of-steel-bowie-knife.html

O'Shea, Henry George (1889) *O'Shea's Guide to Spain and Portugal*

Rivera, Tim. (2016) *Iberian Swordplay – Domingo Luis Godinho's Art of Fencing (Arte de esgrima) 1599* Wheaton, IL: Freelance Academy Press.

Scott, Samuel Parsons (1886) *Through Spain: a Narrative of Travel and Adventure in the Peninsula*

Smith, Michael & Ingelmo, Luis (2012) *Cantes Flamencos*

Notable authors for Iberian fencing:

Jaime Pons de Perpiñan (~1474)

Domingo Luis Godinho (1599) (translation by Tim Rivera 2016)

Diogo Gomes de Figueyredo (1628, 1651)

Jerónimo Sánchez de Carranza (1582)

Luis Pacheco de Narvaez (1600, 1608, 1625, 1632, 1635, 1639)

Gérard Thibault d'Anvers (1630)

ABOUT THE AUTHOR

James Wran has trained in numerous martial arts since the age of 8, and has been an instructor for over 20 years. He holds Black Belt ranks in a number of Eastern Martial Arts.

James has trained in HEMA (Historical European Martial Arts) since 2000. With friend and author Henry Walker, he opened School of Historical Defence Arts in 2007. He continues the instruction of Italian Longsword, Renaissance and Elizabethan Rapier traditions with Brisbane Swords, Australia.

www.ingramcontent.com/pod-product-compliance
Lightning Source LLC
Chambersburg PA
CBHW031436160426
43195CB00010BB/749